ROUGH GUIDES

T0001621

POCKET **ROUGH GUIDE**

ORKNEY

written and researched by
OWEN MORTON

CONTENTS

Introduction   4

What's new?..5
When to visit..6
Orkney at a glance 8
Things not to miss...................................10

Places   23

Stromness and around..............................24
West Mainland..32
Hoy, South Walls and Flotta.....................44
Kirkwall...56
Burray and South Ronaldsay.....................66
Rousay, Egilsay and Wyre..........................74
Westray and Papa Westray........................81
Northern Isles..92

Accommodation   111

Essentials   119

Arrival 120
Getting around...121
Directory A-Z..122
Festivals and events................................126
Chronology...127
Language 129

A note to readers

At Rough Guides, we always strive to bring you the most up-to-date information. This book was produced during a period of continuing uncertainty caused by the Covid-19 pandemic, so please note that content is more subject to change than usual. We recommend checking the latest restrictions and official guidance.

ORKNEY

An archipelago scattered across the North Sea around ten miles north of Scotland, Orkney is a unique destination. Best known for the remarkable prehistoric village of Skara Brae and the strategic importance of its vast harbour in the two World Wars, Orkney could easily preoccupy visitors for a month. Boasting attractions that range from world-beating neolithic sites to gorgeous coastal scenery, via outstanding wildlife-watching and excellent restaurants, it's easy for Orkney to cast its spell. The archipelago may take a little effort to reach, but visitors who make the effort are richly rewarded.

Old croft ruins in Orphir with view of Hoy in the distance

Though Orkney is made up of about seventy islands, only twenty of them are inhabited. Out of a total population of 22,000, the vast majority (17,000 people) live on Mainland – the largest of Orkney's islands – mostly in the larger towns, Kirkwall and Stromness. The other islands are divided into groups known as the North Isles and the South Isles, which are variously home to settlements ranging in size from Westray's reasonably large Pierowall to South Walls' tiny Longhope.

Orkney has an extraordinarily long history. The archipelago has been inhabited for at least 5500 years, and possibly for up to 3000 years prior to that. The prehistoric people who lived here left considerable remains, making Orkney one of the most archeologically significant places in Europe: many sites date back to the neolithic period (around 4000 BC–1700 BC) – older than the Egyptian Pyramids. Tourists flock to the big-hitters from this era, including the fascinating remains of the village of Skara Brae and the atmospheric Ring of Brodgar, but there are many lesser-known but similarly intriguing neolithic sites that reward a visit, including Northern Europe's oldest stone house, the Knap of Howar, which dates to 3700 BC.

The neolithic period gave way to the Iron Age, which saw another wave of construction: this was the

Fishing boat at Stromness Harbour

era of the broch, strong towers often built in strategic coastal locations. It's not known who built the brochs, though differing schools of thought suggest either the descendants of the neolithic islanders or newcomers such as the Picts. What is certain is that by around the sixth century, Orkney was part of the Pictish kingdom, a period characterized by relative peace and stability.

This changed in the ninth century, when the islands became part of the Norse kingdom, and so began the so-called Viking Age.

What's new?

Orkney's major new tourist attraction is the Scapa Flow Museum (see page 49), focused on the wartime history of the Scapa Flow naval base. This museum reopened in July 2022 after several years' renovation, with snazzy new virtual-reality exhibits, interactive displays and plenty of room to show off many items in the museum's collection that have never been seen by the public before.

A more wide-ranging newcomer on the scene is the digital initiative, History of Orkney Islands, which launched in 2022. Buy a ticket online to any of Historic Environment's Orkney sites (ⓦ historicenvironment.scot), and you'll be granted access to digital tours of 35 historic attractions, giving you a wide overview of the islands' heritage, even if you can't physically visit every spot.

Much of the history of Orkney under the Norse is told in the Orkneyinga Saga, which celebrates the deeds of the many powerful earls who ruled the islands in this period. The most significant, perhaps, is the tale of Earl Magnus, apparently a wise and gentle earl who was betrayed by his cousin and beheaded. Very soon, miracles were reported at the site of his martyrdom, and he was declared a saint in 1135. His remains were transferred to St Magnus Cathedral in Kirkwall, now the northernmost cathedral in the UK.

Orkney became part of the Scottish kingdom in 1472, and part of the Kingdom of Great Britain following the Act of Union in 1707. During the Jacobite revolts in the eighteenth century, the islands were one of the last holdouts of the rebels, and you'll still come across parts of the coastline – for example, around Westray's Noup Head – that were once the hideouts of Jacobite rebels.

The vast natural harbour of Scapa Flow made Orkney an ideal base for Britain's large navy, and so Orkney assumed considerable strategic importance during both World Wars. During the early stages of World War II, the harbour was breached by an enemy submarine which managed to sink the British battleship *HMS Royal Oak*. In response, UK Prime Minister Winston Churchill ordered the construction of the Churchill Barriers, an enormous engineering project that blocked the eastern approaches to Scapa Flow, resulting in the linking of Orkney's Mainland to the southern islands of Burray and South Ronaldsay.

Orkney's economy today is mainly centred on agriculture, with most of its land used for grazing sheep and cattle. Tourism also plays an important part, with visitors keen to explore everything Orkney has to offer, from the islands' rich history to pristine beaches, wildlife-watching opportunities and gorgeous coastal walks. With all this and more, it would be easy to visit for two weeks and still barely scratch the surface of this unique destination.

When to visit

Orkney enjoys a fairly mild climate year-round: given its far north location, it rarely experiences enormously high temperatures, but spring, summer and early autumn are generally pleasant – though you should be prepared for rainy and cloudy weather at any time. By contrast, even in the depths of winter, the islands never get dispiritingly cold, though they can be relentlessly grey and blasted by high winds for days on end. The summer is the most popular time to visit, and throughout peak season, accommodation and restaurants can get booked up, and you may have to plan considerably in advance to get a ticket to top attractions like Maeshowe. That said, Orkney rarely feels crowded, except at the very popular tourist sites – and even then, with a bit of planning and knowledge of when cruise ships dock at Kirkwall, you can avoid the busiest times. In general, June to August are probably the best months to come, but visiting in April, May or September is also a good choice. Outside this period, many attractions close and most restaurants have reduced opening times, but if you're looking for solitude, the winter can still be a rewarding time to visit.

Where to...

Shop

Orkney is home to a thriving crafts industry, and across the islands, you'll see signs for little independent shops selling all manner of goods, from clothing and jewellery to furniture and ornaments. The island of Stronsay has a remarkably high concentration of **craft shops**, but there are plenty of excellent places on almost all the islands. Stromness is especially worth exploring if you're looking for artwork, as there is a clutch of excellent **art galleries** here. Locally produced food and drink is perhaps best sourced in Kirkwall, which is dotted with delis selling cheese, fish, whisky and much more besides. Souvenir shops can be found in many places, particularly Kirkwall and Stromness, and in the heritage centres on several of the islands, notably Sanday and Westray.

OUR FAVOURITES: Harray Potter, see page 42. The Brig Larder, see page 62. Hume Sweet Hume, see page 90. Wheeling Steen Gallery, see page 90.

Eat

Orkney prides itself on its local produce, of which there is a fine and varied selection. It's no surprise that, as a group of islands, Orkney is best known for fish and seafood – Orkney scallops, crab and lobster are regularly found on menus, and are usually excellent. Fish'n'chips is a popular option, often found on pub menus or in smaller takeaway places. Meat-eaters will enjoy the delicious Orkney beef, and on South Ronaldsay, there's the opportunity to try the native mutton. Vegetarians are always catered for, though, in some cases, options are not particularly imaginative: macaroni cheese is a common option. Another popular choice is the local Grimbister cheese, which is usually deep-fried. **Kirkwall** offers the most cosmopolitan selection of **restaurants**, while other towns and villages are rather more limited, so you may need to take picnics – several of the islands have nowhere to eat at all, and there's a surprisingly small number of places to eat in Stromness.

OUR FAVOURITES: The Merkister, see page 42. Twenty One, see page 63. Polly Kettle, see page 73. 59° North, see page 108.

Drink

Traditional pubs are something of a rarity in Orkney, though a couple of drinking dens are scattered throughout the islands, and more than a few on **Mainland**. **Kirkwall** is home to several good choices, at which you'll be able to sample local beers, whiskies and – perhaps unexpectedly – rum. Orkney is also home to a smattering of excellent cafés, many of which offer great coffee, though in many cases, opening hours are limited to a few days a week. It's always worth double-checking opening times if you have your heart set on a place.

OUR FAVOURITES: Helgi's, see page 64. Robertsons Coffee Hoose, see page 73. Richans Retreat, see page 91.

Orkney at a glance

Westray and Papa Westray p.81.
Westray offers gorgeous beaches and fine birdwatching opportunities, while Papa Westray is home to one of Orkney's most significant prehistoric sites, the Knap of Howar.

Rousay, Egilsay and Wyre p.74.
Visit Rousay's huge concentration of archeological sites, including the beautiful Midhowe Broch and the atmospheric Knowe of Yarso Cairn, as well as Egilsay's historically significant St Magnus Church.

West Mainland p.32.
Many of Orkney's top archeological sites are found here, including the evocative Ring of Brodgar, the Standing Stones of Stenness, and the haunting Maeshowe tomb.

Stromness and around p.24.
Visit the pretty town of Stromness, then head out to the Unesco-listed prehistoric village of Skara Brae, followed by exploring rugged coastal scenery at Yesnaby.

Hoy, South Walls and Flotta p.44.
Take in a walk to one of Orkney's most iconic viewpoints overlooking the Old Man of Hoy sea stack, before having a wander along South Wall's gorgeous coastline.

Noup

Wes

Rousay

Wasb

We

Brough Head
Birsay
Swannay

Evie

Twatt

Tir

Dounby

Keldabra

Hackland

Appietown
Finstown

Westfield

Stromness
Stenness
Mair

Graemsay

Houton

Linksness
Cava   Sc

Rackwick

Fara

Hoy

Flotta

Lyness

Longhope
Swith

South
Walls

Swona

Pentland F

ATLANTIC
OCEAN

Stroma

Dunnet
Head

Gill's   John
Bay   O'Groa

Scrabster
Thurso
Dunnet

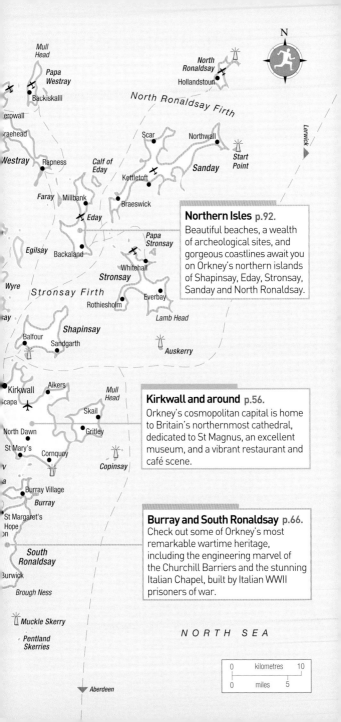

N

Mull
Head

*Papa
Westray*

Backiskalll

North
Ronaldsay

Hollandstoun

North Ronaldsay Firth

Lerwick

erowall

raehead

Westray

Rapness

*Calf of
Eday*

Scar

Northwall

Kettletoft

Start
Point

Sanday

Faray Millbank

Braeswick

Egilsay Backaland

Eday

*Papa
Stronsay*

Whitehall

Stronsay

Wyre Stronsay Firth

Everbay

say

Rothiesholm

Lamb Head

Shapinsay

Balfour
Sandgarth

Auskerry

Northern Isles p.92.

Beautiful beaches, a wealth of archeological sites, and gorgeous coastlines await you on Orkney's northern islands of Shapinsay, Eday, Stronsay, Sanday and North Ronaldsay.

Kirkwall Aikers

capa

North Dawn

St Mary's

Cornquoy

*Mull
Head*

Skail

Gritley

Copinsay

Kirkwall and around p.56.

Orkney's cosmopolitan capital is home to Britain's northernmost cathedral, dedicated to St Magnus, an excellent museum, and a vibrant restaurant and café scene.

Burray Village

Burray

St Margaret's
Hope
n

*South
Ronaldsay*

Burwick

Brough Ness

Burray and South Ronaldsay p.66.

Check out some of Orkney's most remarkable wartime heritage, including the engineering marvel of the Churchill Barriers and the stunning Italian Chapel, built by Italian WWII prisoners of war.

Muckle Skerry

*Pentland
Skerries*

NORTH   SEA

0	kilometres	10
0	miles	5

Aberdeen

15 Things not to miss

It's not possible to see everything that Orkney has to offer in one trip – and we don't suggest you try. What follows is a curation of Orkney's highlights, from neolithic remains and wartime heritage to unspoiled beaches and serene coastal walks.

> **Old Man of Hoy**
> **See page 48**
> Take a bracing coastal walk to one of Orkney's most iconic sights: the imposing 137m-tall Old Man of Hoy sea stack.

< **Skara Brae**
  See page 27
  The astonishing prehistoric village of Skara Brae is one of the best-preserved neolithic monuments in the world.

∨ **Italian Chapel**
  See page 66
  A beautiful expression of creativity and devotion by artistic Italian prisoners of war, the Italian Chapel is a unique piece of wartime heritage.

‹ Sanday's beaches
See page 103
Fine white sand, turquoise waters
dappled by sunlight – no, you're
not in the Caribbean, but on
the island of Sanday, whose
name holds a clue to the nature
of its coastline.

⌄ Midhowe Broch
See page 76
The island of Rousay holds many
archeological treasures, but
perhaps the finest is Midhowe
Broch, a 2000-year-old tower built
in a sublime coastal spot.

< Ring of Brodgar
See page 36
One of the largest and most idyllically situated stone circles in Britain, the Ring of Brodgar has stood for 4500 years as a monument to the beliefs and rituals of its prehistoric makers.

∨ Noup Head Lighthouse
See page 86
The walk along rugged coastal paths to Noup Head Lighthouse offers gorgeous scenery and the chance to see a wide variety of seabirds.

∧ **St Magnus Cathedral**
See page 56
Britain's northernmost cathedral is a beautiful building, composed of local red and yellow sandstone, and dedicated to Orkney's most beloved saint.

< **Vat of Kirbuster**
See page 99
Strike out along Stronsay's cliff paths to the Vat of Kirbuster – an impressive rock arch – and ponder the power of the ocean.

∧ Diving in Scapa Flow
See page 49
Get up close and personal with the sunken wrecks of the German fleet, scuttled in Scapa Flow in 1919 in the aftermath of World War I.

∨ Maeshowe
See page 33
Of the many burial mounds in Orkney, Maeshowe is the most striking: visit and marvel at the skill involved in building this perfect stone tomb.

∧ **Longhope
Lifeboat Museum**

See page 50

Learn the history of Orkney's dedicated lifeboat team, and admire the *Thomas McCunn* lifeboat, which was in service from 1933 until 1962 and now takes pride of place in the museum.

< **Churchill Barriers**

See page 67

Born of wartime necessity, the Churchill Barriers are an engineering marvel and a unique example of World War II heritage.

< Knap of Howar
See page 87
Explore Northern Europe's oldest stone house, the Knap of Howar, which is potentially over 5500 years old.

∨ Birdwatching on North Ronaldsay
See page 106
The small island of North Ronaldsay is an important stop on migratory routes – perfect for birdwatching trips.

THINGS NOT TO MISS

Day one in Orkney

Skara Brae. See page 27. Any trip to Orkney has to begin with its most famous sight, Skara Brae, a remarkably well-preserved prehistoric village. Explore this archeological treasure, before visiting the adjacent Skaill House for a taste of more modern history.

Yesnaby Castle. See page 25. Take a short walk along the stunning wind-sculpted scenery just south of Skara Brae, visiting the teetering sea stack known as Yesnaby Castle.

🍴 **Lunch.** See page 31. Head into Stromness and enjoy a light meal at *Julia's Café*, or pick up supplies for a picnic from the excellent *Bayleaf Delicatessen*.

Maeshowe. See page 33. Time for another of Orkney's top tourist sights: Maeshowe, an enormous and atmospheric prehistoric tomb, where you can't help but marvel at the skill of its neolithic builders.

Evie Beach. See page 39. If it's sunny, the golden sand and blue waters of Evie Beach are just as beautiful as anywhere in the Caribbean. If the weather isn't working in your favour, check out the nearby archeological site of the Broch of Gurness.

🍴 **Dinner.** See page 42. Excellent food and gorgeous views over the Loch of Harray await at the *Merkister Hotel*, or grab a takeaway wood-fired pizza from *Eviedale Bistro* to share on the beach.

Ring of Brodgar. See page 36. Finish the day at the evocative Ring of Brodgar; time your visit for sunset to see the stones silhouetted against the orange sky. Though its precise age is unknown, archeologists have guessed that it dates back about 4500 years.

Skara Brae

Yesnaby Castle

Eviedale Bistro

Day two in Orkney

Castle o'Burrian. See page 81. It's an early start for the ferry to Westray; once you're on the island, head to Castle o'Burrian to enjoy a coastal walk and spot puffins nesting on the cliffs.

Pierowall. See page 85. Visit Westray's main settlement, the village of Pierowall, and check out the outstanding Westray Heritage Centre to learn the fascinating history of the island via a selection of remarkable artefacts.

Lunch. See page 91. *Saintear*, just outside Pierowall, is one of the island's best places for a delicious lunch. Fuel up with a hearty sandwich and soup, but be sure to save room for one of the excellent cakes.

Noltland Castle. See page 85. Explore the labyrinthine passageways and marvel at the outsized staircase of this well-preserved fortress, built by the unpopular Sir Gilbert Balfour in the sixteenth century.

Grobust Beach. See page 86. One of Orkney's prettiest beaches, Grobust boasts a wide expanse of white sand and is perfect for a seaside stroll. The Links of Noltland, behind the beach, is an important archeological site.

Noup Head. See page 86. Take a circular walk to Noup Head Lighthouse for dramatic clifftop scenery and the chance to spot nesting seabirds.

Dinner. See page 91. If you're staying overnight on Westray, linger over a meal at the *Pierowall Hotel*, or return on the evening ferry to Kirkwall and choose from the many restaurants in town. Try *Dil Se* for Indian cuisine, *Lucano* for Italian classics or *Twenty One* for an exciting globe-trotting menu.

Puffin at Castle o'Burrian

Beach on Papa Westray

Noup Head Lighthouse

Wartime Orkney

Orkney was a hugely strategic location in both the World Wars, and plenty of fascinating and unexpectedly varied wartime heritage remains on the islands.

The Churchill Barriers. See page 67. The Churchill Barriers are among Orkney's most significant pieces of wartime heritage. Built to safeguard Scapa Flow's harbour, the Barriers now link Mainland with a string of southern islands.

Italian Chapel. See page 66. Italian prisoners of war interned on the island of Lamb Holm found an outlet for their creativity in the design and construction of the astonishing Italian Chapel, which is dedicated to the ideal of peace.

Hackness Martello Tower and Battery. See page 51. Built to defend Longhope Sound, the Hackness Martello Tower and Battery can now be visited on a fascinating guided tour.

Diving in Scapa Flow. See page 49. In 1919, the German fleet was scuttled in Scapa Flow, and seven ships remain beneath the surface here. Take a diving trip to explore these century-old wrecks.

Museums. A handful of museums across the islands offers an excellent introduction to the war years in Orkney: try the Scapa Flow Museum on Hoy (see page 49) or the Orkney Fossil and Heritage Centre on Burray (see page 67).

Flotta. See page 53. Wartime remains can be found on most of Orkney's islands, but small and often-overlooked Flotta has one of the greatest and most varied concentrations of wartime sites. On the east coast, check out Buchanan Battery and the extensive, scenically located Stanger Battery, while near the ferry port, you'll find the remains of the wartime cinema that was built for troops stationed here.

Churchill Barrier No 3

Italian Chapel

Buchanan Battery, Flotta

Budget Orkney

Enjoy Orkney without breaking the bank by visiting free attractions, eating picnics, travelling on interisland ferries, and wild camping at night.

Historic Orkney. Although some of the top Orkney sights (for example, Skara Brae and Maeshowe) charge for entry, most historic sites don't cost a penny. The Ring of Brodgar, the Stones of Stenness and Wideford Hill Cairn (see pages 36, 33 and 40) are good choices on Mainland, while Rousay's southwest coastline is littered with free archeological sites. Plus, most museums do not charge entry fees – Kirkwall's Orkney Museum (see page 56) is particularly good.

The Iron Age Broch of Gurness

Walking. Orkney is blessed with some magnificent scenery, and it's entirely free to explore. Particularly fine routes include Westray's Noup Head circuit (see page 87), the Eday Heritage Trail (see page 97), the Mull Head circular (see page 61), and of course the out-and-back route to the iconic Old Man of Hoy (see page 48).

Wildlife spotting. Wherever you go in Orkney, you're likely to spot wildlife along the way. Inland, you've got a great chance of seeing species such as hares and short-eared owls, while along the coastline, you'll find seabirds aplenty and often seals, too. If you're lucky, you might glimpse the magnificent orca, a reasonably frequent summer visitor to Orkney's waters.

Seals on North Ronaldsay

Picnics. There's no need to shell out to eat at cafés and restaurants when you could opt for a picnic instead. Swing by excellent shops like *The Brig Larder* (see page 62) or the *Bayleaf Delicatessen* (see page 30) to choose supplies for an alfresco meal along the coast or on the shores of the Loch of Harray.

Fresh crab picnic on Rackwick Beach

PLACES

Stromness and around.............................**24**

West Mainland...**32**

Hoy, South Walls and Flotta...................**44**

Kirkwall **56**

Burray and South Ronaldsay.................**66**

Rousay, Egilsay and Wyre **74**

Westray and Papa Westray.....................**81**

Northern Isles...**92**

Stromness

Stromness and around

Most visitors to Orkney will arrive via the passenger ferry that reaches Stromness from Scrabster on the mainland. One of Orkney's two main towns, Stromness is a pretty little place, consisting primarily of one winding main street that threads along close to the harbourside. It is home to a fascinating museum, a highly regarded art gallery, plenty of good shops and a decent pub. Better still, it's within easy reach of one of Orkney's top sights, the prehistoric village of Skara Brae, which is less than fifteen minutes' drive away. Add in the rugged coastline at Yesnaby, and it's easy to see why you'd want to linger in this corner of Orkney.

Stromness Museum

MAP PAGE 26
52 Alfred St, KW16 3DH
Ⓦ stromnessmuseum.org.uk. Mon–Sat 10am–1pm & 1.45–5pm (Wed till 7pm), Sun 11am–4pm. Charge.

An excellent and extensive collection awaits you in the charmingly old-school **Stromness Museum**, covering the history of both Stromness and Orkney as a whole. Don't just look at eye level – there are exhibits high and low. With model ships perched on top of cabinets, and a whale skull partially concealed beneath a table, it's a marvellously rambling place.

The maritime history section, covering shipwrecks, whaling and the scuttling of the German fleet, is particularly strong, and the exhibition on John Rae's expedition to the Northwest Passage is fascinating. Natural history also gets a good look-in, with stuffed examples of much of Orkney's wildlife. While it's hard not to feel sorry for all these taxidermied creatures, it must be admitted that it's nice to be able to get a good look at a skua without worrying it's going to divebomb you.

For archeology fiends, the top exhibit has to be the Skara Brae 'buddo' figure, which occupies a small case near the entrance. This exquisite 9.5cm-tall whalebone-carved figurine was originally found in a dig at Skara Brae in the late nineteenth century. It then went on display in Edinburgh, but its location from the 1920s onward was unknown until it was rediscovered in 2016 in a box in the museum's store.

A short walk south of the museum is Login's Well, from which numerous ships drew water over the centuries. Perhaps the

Statue of Arctic explorer John Rae

Notable residents

Stromness has a couple of claims to fame. Notable residents of the town include Eliza Fraser, who was shipwrecked on the Great Barrier Reef in 1836 and spent some time among the First Nations Australians, subsequently claiming without apparent truth that they had ill-treated her. Stromness also adopted Arctic explorer John Rae as its own, despite the fact that he was actually born in the nearby village of Orphir. Nonetheless, a bronze statue dedicated to the Scottish surgeon takes pride of place on the harbourfront, from where he set sail in 1833 bound for Canada.

most famous ships to use it were Captain Cook's HMS *Resolution* and HMS *Discovery* in 1780, on their first British landfall since leaving Hawaii.

Pier Arts Centre

MAP PAGE 26
Victoria St, KW16 3AA Ⓦ pierartscentre.com. Mon–Sat 10.30am–5pm. Free.
Housing a small but significant collection of largely abstract artwork and sculpture, the **Pier Arts Centre** was established in the 1970s by Margaret Gardiner, an influential supporter of the St Ives school of artists in the inter-war and post-war years. Alongside the permanent display, temporary exhibitions are frequently hosted here – check the website for details of what's on during your visit. There's a small gift shop that, among other souvenirs, sells an impressive selection of art-focused books and prints of some of the works in the collection.

Ness Battery

MAP PAGE 28
Guardhouse Park, KW16 3DP
Ⓦ nessbattery.co.uk. Daily, by guided tour only; check website for times. Charge.
An important installation defending Scapa Flow during the World Wars, the **Ness Battery** was decommissioned in the 1950s and is now open for excellent guided tours. Visitors can explore the gun emplacements, check out the original World War II accommodation huts, and admire the impressive mural depicting rural England in the mess hall – thought to have been painted by some of the troops garrisoned there as a reminder of home.

Note that mapping apps suggest that you reach the battery by driving along a footpath from Netherton Rd: this is not a route suitable for vehicles, and you should instead approach along the private road through the golf course. The footpath in question, however, does offer tremendous views across to Hoy, so if you have time after visiting the battery, it's a good place for a short wander.

Orkney Folklore and Storytelling Centre

MAP PAGE 28
A967, nr Stromness, KW16 3JF
Ⓦ orkneystorytelling.com. Visits by prior arrangement. Charge.
Dedicated to preserving the oral heritage of Orkney, the **Folklore and Storytelling Centre** runs a programme of events in which traditional tales are regaled to visitors as they sit by the fire. There's also a small folk art studio and gallery, and a fascinating archive of Orkney heritage material, including old photographs and newspapers. Prebooking is essential.

Yesnaby Castle

MAP PAGE 28
A stretch of rugged and dramatic coastal scenery will be your reward if you take the easy

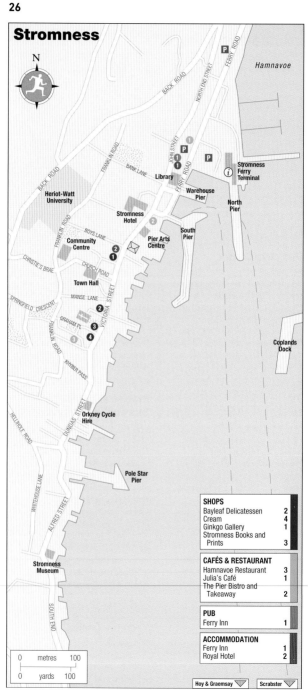

Stromness

N

Hamnavoe

FERRY ROAD

BACK ROAD

NORTH END STREET

JOHN STREET

FERRY ROAD

Stromness Ferry Terminal

i

Library

Warehouse Pier

North Pier

FRANKLIN ROAD

BANK LANE

BACK ROAD

Heriot-Watt University

Stromness Hotel

BOYS LANE

Pier Arts Centre

South Pier

Community Centre

FRANKLIN ROAD

CHRISTIE'S BRAE

CHURCH ROAD

Town Hall

SPRINGFIELD CRESCENT

MANSE LANE

VICTORIA STREET

GRAHAM PL

FRANKLIN ROAD

KIRK PASS

Coplands Dock

HELLIHOLE ROAD

DUNDAS STREET

Orkney Cycle Hire

WHITEHOUSE LANE

Pole Star Pier

ALFRED STREET

Stromness Museum

SOUTH END

SHOPS	
Bayleaf Delicatessen	2
Cream	4
Ginkgo Gallery	1
Stromness Books and Prints	3

CAFÉS & RESTAURANT	
Hamnavoe Restaurant	3
Julia's Café	1
The Pier Bistro and Takeaway	2

PUB	
Ferry Inn	1

ACCOMMODATION	
Ferry Inn	1
Royal Hotel	2

0 metres 100

0 yards 100

Hoy & Graemsay ▽   Scrabster ▽

Diving in Scapa Flow

Orkney is a world-renowned diving destination, in no small part due to the remains of the German World War I fleet, which was scuttled here in 1919. There are seven wrecks remaining beneath the surface of Scapa Flow, which offer the chance for a fascinating exploration. Numerous diving outlets in Orkney – most of them based in Stromness – can arrange diving trips for beginners and experienced divers alike. Of these, Kraken Diving (ⓦ krakendiving.co.uk) has a particularly good reputation, but you can check out ⓦ orkney.com/things/leisure/diving for further listings.

footpath south from the car park at the end of Yesnaby Road, about five miles north of Stromness. The coastline here is jagged, contoured by fjord-like inlets; following the trail, after about twenty minutes, you'll reach a dramatic rock arch. Just around the corner from here is **Yesnaby Castle** itself, not actually a castle but a gorgeous sea stack supported by two rock struts, forming a mini arch in its base. This is an easy out-and-back walk that gives a great taste of Orkney's rugged coastline.

Skara Brae

MAP PAGE 28
Sandwick, KW16 3LR
ⓦ historicenvironment.scot/visit-a-place/places/skara-brae. Daily: April–Sept 9.30am–5.30pm; Oct–March 10am–4pm. Charge (ticket also includes entry to Skaill House).

Mention Orkney in conversation and it won't be long before **Skara Brae** comes up: this remarkable archeological site is unquestionably Orkney's best-known attraction. A Stone Age village dating back more than five thousand years – older than Stonehenge and the Pyramids – this collection of at least ten buildings was buried beneath the sand until 1850, when it was unearthed by a storm. Subsequently excavated a series of times over the nineteenth and twentieth centuries, Skara Brae village now offers a fascinating insight into the everyday lives of Stone Age people.

Your visit begins with an excellent exhibition, which presents examples of artefacts found here, including pots, finely decorated jewellery, and some whalebone objects that may be dice. There's even a small sample of a midden – a domestic rubbish heap – which the inhabitants recycled for further use. Just outside the visitor centre is a reconstructed house, which gives a great impression of how the settlement may have looked in its heyday. It contains replica items including pots, shelves and a small boat.

From here, you walk along a path – interspersed with stones

Yesnaby Castle sea stack

Stromness and around

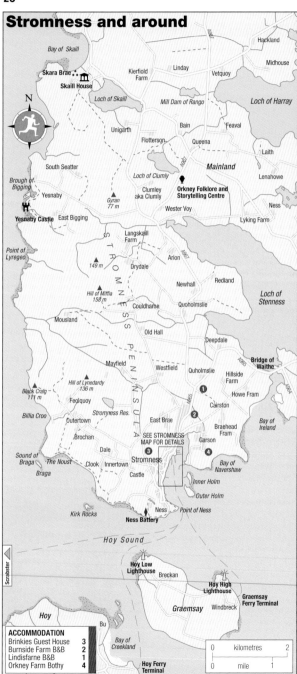

Bay of Skaill

Hackland

Midhouse

Skara Brae

Skaill House

Kierfield Farm

Linday

Vetquoy

Loch of Skaill

Mill Dam of Rango

Loch of Harray

N

Unigarth

Flotterson

Bain

Feaval

Queena

Laith

Mainland

Lenahowe

South Seatter

Loch of Clumly

Orkney Folklore and Storytelling Centre

Ness

Brough of Bigging

Yesnaby

East Bigging

Clumley aka Clumly

Wester Voy

Lyking Farm

Yesnaby Castle

Gyran 77 m

Point of Lyregeo

Langskaill Farm

149 m

Drydale

Arion

Newhall

Redland

Loch of Stenness

Hill of Miffia 158 m

Couldhame

Quoholmslie

Mousland

Old Hall

Deepdale

Bridge of Waithe

Mayfield

Westfield

Quoholmslie

Hillside Farm

Howe Fram

Hill of Lynedardy 136 m

Cairston

Bay of Ireland

Black Craig 111 m

Feolquoy

Stromness Res.

East Brae

Braehead Fram

Billia Croo

Outertown

Garson

Brochan

Dale

SEE STROMNESS MAP FOR DETAILS

Bay of Navershaw

Sound of Braga

The Noust

Clook

Innertown

Stromness

Kirk Rocks

Castle

Inner Holm

Braga

Outer Holm

Ness Battery

Ness

Point of Ness

Hoy Sound

Scrabster

Hoy Low Lighthouse

Breckan

Hoy High Lighthouse

Graemsay Ferry Terminal

Graemsay

Windbreck

Hoy

Bu

ACCOMMODATION
Brinkies Guest House	3
Burnside Farm B&B	2
Lindisfarne B&B	1
Orkney Farm Bothy	4

Bay of Creekland

Hoy Ferry Terminal

0 kilometres 2

0 mile 1

Skara Brae, with Skaill House in the distance

etched with dates of historic events, creating the sense of walking back in time – to the village itself, which occupies a gorgeous spot above Skaill Beach. The path continues around the settlement, offering a bird's-eye view into each house. Structure Number 1 is a particularly good example of how the houses were laid out, with a firepit, beds and a 'dresser' still in evidence. Number 5 is another interesting example, including niches built into the walls that were likely used for storage. Also be sure to check out Number 8, which was a workshop rather than a house.

There's a decent gift shop here stocked with Orkney-themed merchandise, and a good café.

Skaill House

MAP PAGE 28
Sandwick, KW16 3LR ⓦ skaillhouse.co.uk.
Daily: April–Sept 9.30am–5.30pm; Oct–March 10am–4pm. Charge (included with Skara Brae ticket).

Parts of **Skaill House** date back to 1620, though the manor has been extended over the centuries. It's been owned by twelve generations of the same family since its construction, and visitors can explore its rooms, filled with an eclectic collection of artefacts spanning the house's 400-year history, from Skara Brae archeological finds to nineteenth-century Japanese memorabilia.

The dining room is still set with the crockery used when the then-Queen Mother visited in 1983, and also on display is a dinner service thought to have belonged to Captain Cook. Look out, too, for the revolving bookcase in the library, which has more than a touch of *Scooby-Doo* about it. Meanwhile, there's a fabulous cabinet in the main hall that, legend has it, was carved from the wood of El Gran Grifón, a galleon that was wrecked in the aftermath of the Spanish Armada.

Upstairs, notable items include an impressive tiger-skin rug, a collection of rather unpleasant porcelain figures, and – in the Bishop's Bedroom – a fantastic model of Kirkwall's St Magnus Cathedral. There's a good gift shop at the exit, with a fine array of Orkney souvenirs, including bottles of Skaill House's own gin.

Shops

Bayleaf Delicatessen

MAP PAGE 26
103 Victoria St, KW16 3BU
Ⓦ facebook.com/bayleafdelicatessen.
Daily 10am–5.30pm.

Dinky but well-stocked shop that's handy for self-caterers, with plenty of local produce on the shelves. The fish selection, much of which comes from Pierowall on Westray, is particularly good, though you'll also find cheese, cakes, gin and more.

Cream

MAP PAGE 26
23 Graham Pl, KW16 3BY
Ⓦ creamorkney.bigcartel.com.
Mon–Tues, Thurs–Sat 10am–5pm.

A little boutique on Stromness' main street, *Cream* sells a variety of upmarket souvenirs, including lovely art prints, attractive kitchenware, jewellery, and much more. It's a great place to pick up something to take home with you.

Ginkgo Gallery

MAP PAGE 26
59 Victoria St, KW16 3BY

Ⓦ ginkgogalleryorkney.co.uk.
Tues–Wed, Fri & Sat 11am–4pm.

This friendly gallery sells lovely works by local artist Jeanne Bouza Rose and photographer Susan Shackleton, as well as pieces by guest artists. Well worth a browse.

Stromness Books and Prints

MAP PAGE 26
3 Graham Pl, KW16 3BY
Ⓦ stromnessbooksandprints.wordpress.
com. Tues–Sat 2–6pm.

You'll be astounded at just how many books are packed into this tiny shop. Alongside a very strong selection of Orkney-themed titles, there's also a good range of fiction and non-fiction for adults and children alike.

Restaurant

Hamnavoe Restaurant

MAP PAGE 26
35 Graham Pl, KW16 3BY Ⓣ 01856 850606
Ⓦ hamnavoe-restaurant.co.uk.
Wed–Sat 5–10pm.

A great little restaurant offering tasty local food with a Korean twist

Looking towards Hamnavoe Restaurant

The Pier Bistro and Takeaway

– think Orkney lobster with soy, ginger and spring onion noodles. Desserts are similarly imaginative: chances are you won't find chocolate cremeux served with yuzu and candied sea lettuce anywhere else on Orkney. It's a very welcome addition to Stromness' dining scene, and is also open for takeaways at lunchtime. ££

Cafés

Julia's Café
MAP PAGE 26
Ferry Rd, KW16 3AE ☎ 01856 850904
ⓦ juliascafe.co.uk. Mon–Sat 9.30am–4.30pm, Sun 10am–4.30pm.
This friendly place opposite Stromness' ferry terminal is a good choice for a light lunch of soup and sandwiches, or a mid-afternoon stop for coffee and a cake. It's nicest on a sunny day when you can sit outside, though indoor seating is available too. Ordering can be a little chaotic – you'll need to place your order at the counter and then listen carefully for a shout when your food's ready. £

The Pier Bistro and Takeaway
MAP PAGE 26
22 Victoria St, KW16 3AA ☎ 01856 850753
ⓦ facebook.com/Thepierbistro.
Daily 11am–4pm, Thurs–Sun 5–8pm.
Friendly Stromness spot open for eat-in at lunchtime and takeaways on Thursday to Sunday evenings. The excellent fish and chips is the star of the show, but there are plenty of other choices, including mac and cheese, hunter's chicken, and chilli beef stir-fry. ££

Pub

Ferry Inn
MAP PAGE 26
10 John St, KW16 3AD
ⓦ ferryinn.com.
The *Ferry Inn* serves upmarket options using mostly local produce – Orkney crab and Orkney lamb both feature on the menu. As one of the only places in Stromness where you can get a sit-down evening meal, it gets busy, so you'll need to book several days in advance, particularly in high season. £££

West Mainland

The main calling card of Orkney's West Mainland is its trio of Unesco World Heritage sites: the Ring of Brodgar, the Stones of Stenness and Maeshowe Chambered Cairn, which are among the finest prehistoric remains in Britain and essential stops on any visit to Orkney. But they're not all this western corner of the Mainland has to offer: there are further world-beating archeological sites at the Broch of Gurness and Wideford Hill Cairn; stunning beaches such as Evie; and marvellous coastal scenery at the Brough of Birsay and Marwick Head. With so much to see, you'll need to dedicate several full days to exploring this part of Orkney.

Unstan Chambered Cairn

MAP PAGE 34
Off A965, KW16 3JX
ⓦ historicenvironment.scot/visit-a-place/places/unstan-chambered-cairn.
Open 24hr. Free.

In a lovely setting on the shores of the Loch of Stenness, just a short distance from Stromness, **Unstan Chambered Cairn** is an excellent introduction to the profusion of burial chambers dotting Orkney's landscape. It's an archetypal example – a grassy mound, a low entrance tunnel, and the remainder of the internal divisions inside. Note that the road sign to it really doesn't give you much notice – be prepared to turn abruptly.

Happy Valley

MAP PAGE 34
Bigswell Rd, KW16 3LA. Open 24hr. Free

This little patch of idyllic woodland, crisscrossed by paths and bordered by a babbling brook, is a lovely place for a quick leg-stretch, particularly in spring, when the woods are alive with bluebells. **Happy Valley** was the life's work of Edwin Harrold, who settled here in 1948 and intended the area to be for the enjoyment of all Orcadians. At the entrance gate is a typical nineteenth-century croft house, in which Harrold lived for five decades. Happy Valley is not signposted, so you may need to use a good map or mapping app to find it.

Chambered cairns

The prehistoric people of Orkney left behind many tombs scattered across the islands, a good number of which have now been excavated and can be visited. These cairns are constructed with stone, often with low, narrow passages leading into a larger central chamber, off which are smaller rooms where human remains were interred. After construction, the tombs were covered with earth and turf, resulting in their appearance as grassy mounds. Burials in these cairns were usually accompanied by grave goods of some sort, which were likely to have had ritual significance.

Stones of Stenness

Maeshowe

MAP PAGE 34
Maeshowe Visitor Centre,
Ireland Rd, Stenness, KW16 3LB
ⓦ historicenvironment.scot/visit-a-place/
places/maeshowe-chambered-cairn.
Daily: April–Sept 9.30am–5.30pm;
Oct–March 10am–4pm. Charge.

Of all the many chambered cairns peppered across Orkney's landscape, **Maeshowe** is the showstopper. Surrounded by an ancient ditch and wall, the large mound contains a huge internal chamber, with several smaller rooms off to the sides. Some of the stones involved in the construction weigh nearly three tonnes, and it's humbling to think of the amount of effort and dedication that went into moving such enormous blocks in the far distant past.

Though very few human remains have been found inside, its similarity to other such cairns that did contain remains suggests that it was indeed used for burials. The cairn dates back nearly five thousand years, stars in the Orkneyinga Saga, and was even broken into at one point by Vikings, who left behind a vast collection of runic graffiti, some of which is rather impolite.

Maeshowe can only be visited on a guided tour, which you'll want to book well in advance, as it is very popular and there are, at most, four tours per day. Tickets can be booked on the website.

Stones of Stenness

MAP PAGE 34
B9055, Stenness, KW16 3JY
ⓦ historicenvironment.scot/visit-a-place/
places/stones-of-stenness-circle-and-
henge. Open 24hr. Free.

Poised in an idyllic location on the edge of the Loch of Stenness, the **Stones of Stenness** are one of the most prominent examples of Orkney's neolithic heritage and – along with Maeshowe, the Ring of Brodgar and Skara Brae – are included on Unesco's World Heritage Site list as a group of monuments making up the Heart of Neolithic Orkney.

Only four enormous stones remain out of the original eleven or twelve, which once formed an impressive stone circle at the time of construction. Standing up to six

West Mainland

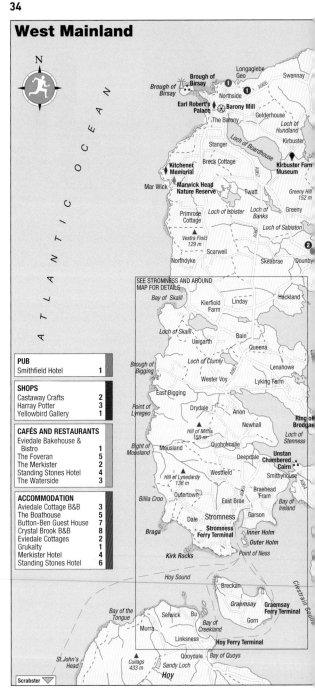

PUB

Smithfield Hotel	1

SHOPS

Castaway Crafts	2
Harray Potter	3
Yellowbird Gallery	1

CAFÉS AND RESTAURANTS

Eviedale Bakehouse & Bistro	1
The Foveran	5
The Merkister	2
Standing Stones Hotel	4
The Waterside	3

ACCOMMODATION

Aviedale Cottage B&B	3
The Boathouse	5
Button-Ben Guest House	7
Crystal Brook B&B	8
Eviedale Cottages	2
Grukalty	1
Merkister Hotel	4
Standing Stones Hotel	6

Costa Head

Eynhallow

Muckle
Water

Ward Hill
190 m

Rousay

Sourin

Costa Hill
151 m

Loch of Swannay

Crismo

Westness
Farm

Peerie
Water

Newhouse

Blotchnie Field
250 m

Brinian

dland Hill
m

Costa

A966

Rymmon

Rousay
Ferry Terminal

Frotoft

Evie Beach

Broch
of Gurness

Howally

Burgar Hill
159 m

Géorth
Farm

Evie

Wyre

Wyre, Egilsay

Skelday Hill
195 m

Mid Hill
193 m

Stenso

Redland

Arwick

The Mello

Eastabist

Woodwick

Burn of Hillside

Hill of Huntis
168 m

Wood Wick

Gairsay Sound

Burn of Grid

eaquoy

Starling Hill
189 m

Hammars Hill
165 m

Tingwall

Tingwall Ferry
Terminal

Fernvalley
Wildlife
Centre

Gairsay

Knarston

Kame of Corrigall
182 m

Milldoe
224 m

Rendall

Breck
House

Rendall
Doocot

Corston

Enzie Hill
141 m

Gorseness

Settiscarth

Keldabrae

Hickland

Ibister

Bay of
Hinderayre

Loch of
Bosquoy

Backkatown

Bay of
Isbister

Bay of
Puldrite

Appietown

Mainland

Burrien Hill
202 m

Burness

Wide Firth

letherbrough

Bimbister

Coubister

Grimeston

Damsay

Quanter
Ness

Moorside

A965

Bay of Firth

Holm of
Grimbister

Saverock

Finstown

ess of
odgar

Maeshowe

Heddle

Grimbister

A965

Wideford
Hill Cairn

Stones of
Stenness

Woodburn

Cuween
Hill

Ingashowe

Wideford Hill
225 m

Blackhill

Kirkwall

Stenness

Germiston

Hill of Lyradale
176 m

Smerquoy

Villasquoy

Happy Valley

Neversdale

Keelylang Hill
221 m

South Rusky
Hill 204 m

Mid Hill
275 m

Mill Bridge

Loch of
Kirbister

Cotland

Clestrain
Cottage

Ward Hill
268 m

Greenigoe

whouse

Gruf Hill
189 m

Hobbister

Hobbister Hill

Petertown

Orphir

Smoogro

Houton

Grindelay

Orkneyinga
Saga Centre

Swanbister Bay

Waulkmill
Bay

Houton Ferry
Terminal

Orphir
Bay
of Myre

Bay

The Breck

Scapa   Flow

Holm of Houton

Lyness   Flotta

| 0 | kilometres | 4 |
| 0 | miles | 2 |

metres high, the quartet makes for an imposing sight. In the centre of the ring was a hearth, and it's thought that the site was used for performing rituals and ceremonies. In the years since the neolithic era, the stones have suffered damage and destruction, most notably in 1814 when a local farmer – apparently fed up with having to plough around them – began to pull them down. His neighbours, dedicated to the preservation of the site, retaliated by attempting twice to burn the farmer's house down. Though Unesco doesn't tend to respond with arson, it is important to be aware that you shouldn't provoke them by damaging the stones.

Ness of Brodgar

MAP PAGE 34
B9055, Stenness, KW16 3JZ
Ⓦ nessofbrodgar.co.uk.
July & Aug Mon–Fri 9.30am–4.30pm. Free.
Draped across a thin strip of land linking the Stones of Stenness with the Ring of Brodgar, the **Ness of Brodgar** was discovered by chance in 2003. Excavations have revealed an extensive village thought to have been an important ceremonial centre. Finds here include some impressive neolithic art, polished stone axes, and ceramics which, in some cases, still hold the fingerprints of the potter who made them. The Ness is only open during excavations in July and August, when free tours of the site run three times a day.

Ring of Brodgar

MAP PAGE 34
B9055, Stenness, KW16 3JZ
Ⓦ historicenvironment.scot/visit-a-place/places/ring-of-brodgar-stone-circle-and-henge. Open 24hr. Free.
One of Orkney's most iconic sights, the **Ring of Brodgar** is an enormous circle composed of thirty-six upright stones, some of them nearly five metres tall. Its precise age is unknown, but archeologists' best guesses suggest that it was erected about 4500 years ago. The 104m-wide circle is ringed by a ditch, or henge, and must have taken a phenomenal amount of work to complete, especially since some of the stones were probably brought here from quarries over six miles away. Set on a finger of land between the lochs of Stenness and Harray, it's a striking, sometimes haunting, place.

Besides the Ring itself, there are a couple of other archeological sites here, including two mounds that may have been tombs, and – a short distance to the south – the Comet Stone, which stands alone outside the circle. It's unknown what its purpose was, but it may have been a marker for a path leading from the Ring of Brodgar to the Stones of Stenness.

Earl Kitchener

Most famous for his stern face looming out of World War I recruitment posters, Horatio Herbert Kitchener – 1st Earl Kitchener – had a successful career in the British Army from 1871 onwards, earning fame in battles from Sudan to South Africa. On the outbreak of war in 1914, he became the Secretary of State for War, in which role he correctly anticipated – against prevailing opinion – that the conflict would not be over quickly. By 1916, he was suffering political attacks over his running of the war effort and his influence was waning, though he retained considerable popular support. Following the sinking of the HMS *Hampshire*, reports of his death were met with grief across the British Empire.

Marwick Head and the Kitchener Memorial

Kitchener Memorial

MAP PAGE 34

In June 1916, Earl Kitchener (see box, page 36), Britain's Secretary of State for War, set sail from Scapa Flow aboard the HMS *Hampshire* on a diplomatic mission to Russia. Just off Marwick Head, the *Hampshire* hit a German mine and sank in less than half an hour, with the loss of most of the ship's complement, including Kitchener; only twelve people survived. A monument was built on Marwick Head in 1926, originally paying tribute only to Kitchener: in 2016, this was amended with the addition of a commemorative wall, bearing the names of all 737 people who died when the *Hampshire* sank.

The 14.5m-tall **Kitchener Memorial** makes an excellent focal point for walks along Marwick Head, which is also a great place for birdwatching – the cliffs beneath the monument are prime nesting spots for species including puffins, guillemots and skuas. From the monument, you'll have views north to the Brough of Birsay, while to the south, you can often make out the Old Man of Hoy.

Earl Robert's Palace

MAP PAGE 34

Birsay, KW17 2LX Ⓦ historicenvironment. scot/visit-a-place/places/earls-palace-birsay. Open 24hr. Free.

The small but atmospheric ruins of **Earl Robert's Palace** are worth a quick stop while you're exploring the northwest corner of the Mainland. Built in the late 1500s by Earl Robert Stewart, an illegitimate half-brother of Mary, Queen of Scots, the once-proud Renaissance structure fell into disrepair from 1700 onwards, but it's still easy to make out the original design, centred around a large courtyard and well, and surrounded by chambers and towers. The west gallery, which was probably servant quarters, is the most complete, while to the north, you'll find the remains of the Great Hall and the main bedchamber.

Brough of Birsay

MAP PAGE 34

Birsay, KW17 2LX Ⓦ historicenvironment. scot/visit-a-place/places/brough-of-birsay. Open 24hr. Free.

Accessible only by causeway at low tide, the small island of the

Broch and roll

A broch is a tower structure that's unique to Scotland: they can be found all over the country, though there's a particular concentration in the far northeast, including Orkney and Shetland. Constructed in the Iron Age, their purpose remains unclear: one theory suggests that they were defensive structures, but archeologists since the 1980s have come to believe that brochs were in fact intended as a display of wealth and status, akin to a stately home.

Brough of Birsay was once a powerful settlement under the Picts and the Norse between the seventh and thirteenth centuries, and many impressive artefacts from this period have been found here.

Immediately upon arrival are the ruins of a small Norse settlement, the most prominent building of which is the ruined church, built in around 1100.

This settlement may have been the home of the Earl of Orkney, Thorfinn the Mighty, who, according to the Orkneyinga Saga, lived at Birsay – though it's uncertain whether the Saga means the Brough or the village on the Mainland.

Broch of Gurness

Once you've explored the remains, take a walk around the perimeter of the island for excellent birdwatching opportunities – puffins, gannets and many more species are often spotted here. It also can be a good place to see orcas.

There is no information on tide times at the car park, so make sure you've checked online or at the *Yellowbird Gallery* (see page 42) before crossing the causeway: if you get marooned, it'll be an uncomfortably long wait until you can return to the Mainland.

Barony Mill

MAP PAGE 34
A967, Birsay, KW17 2LY ⓦ baronymill.com.
Daily April–Sept 11am–5pm. Charge.
Just outside Birsay, the **Barony Mill** was built in 1873 and is still in the business of producing flour today. Engaging guided tours demonstrate the mill's functionality – you may even be allowed to activate the water wheel. A small shop sells the mill's flour and other local produce.

Kirbuster Farm Museum

MAP PAGE 34
Hundland Rd, Birsay, KW17 2LR
ⓣ 01856 771268. Mon–Sat 10am–1pm & 2–5pm, Sun 1–5pm. Free.
The marvellously atmospheric **Kirbuster Farm Museum** is a preserved farm dating back to the 1700s. Inside, you'll find the farmhouse set up as it would have been in days gone by, with different rooms replicating different time

periods. In the oldest room, there's even a genuine peat-burning hearth in action, which means you can smell, as well as see, what life was like in the early eighteenth century. Elsewhere, there's a small but beautiful garden with fine views over the Loch of Boardhouse, and in the barn, you'll discover a well-labelled collection of farm machinery and tools. There are several similar museums across Orkney, but if you only visit one, make it this one.

Evie Beach

MAP PAGE 34

Evie, KW17 2NH. Open 24hr. Free.

Accessed from the road leading to the Broch of Gurness, **Evie** is one of Orkney's prettiest beaches, comprising a wide sandy sweep with views looking across to Rousay. This stretch of water is known as the Eynhallow and was long an important sea route in Iron Age and Viking times. It's thought there were once up to ten brochs lining its shores on either side.

Broch of Gurness

MAP PAGE 34

Evie, KW17 2NH ⓦ historicenvironment. scot/visit-a-place/places/broch-of-gurness. April–Sept Fri–Tues 9.30am–noon, & 1–5pm. Charge.

Unquestionably one of Orkney's archeological big-hitters, **Gurness** is a particularly well-preserved

example of a broch. The tower itself would have once reached up to nine metres tall; it's now reduced to around a third of its original height, but it's still more than possible to get an impression of its earlier scale. Surrounded by a string of ruined buildings that are likely to have formed a small settlement, and protected by defensive ditches and earthworks, it's a must-see for anyone even remotely interested in Orkney's distant past.

You can explore the remains of the houses, where helpful signs point out features such as the hearth, a kiln, a water-storage tank, and an alcove that may have been a toilet. Afterwards, enter the tower itself, where the delineation of internal rooms is clear, as are the beginnings of staircases. Squeeze into the room to the right of the entrance to look at the internal corridor: changes to the uses of the broch over the years, coupled with the nature of the excavation works here, have made it difficult to tell whether this was always accessible from the entranceway, or whether it was originally reached from the interior.

Also on site are the ruins of a small Pictish house, which was built after the broch: it's thought the Picts continued to use the tower after its original inhabitants abandoned it. The Vikings also

John Gow

As you travel around Orkney, you're likely to come across references to John Gow, who enjoyed a short career as a pirate. Born in Stromness in 1698, by November 1724, Gow was serving on a ship called the *Caroline*, where he led a mutiny, killing the captain and assuming command. Renaming the ship, the *Revenge*, he spent the next few months attacking British ships off the Iberian Peninsula, before returning to Orkney in early 1725. After raiding the Hall of Clestrain near Orphir, he attempted to do the same with Carrick House on Eday, but was repelled and ran aground on the Calf of Eday. He was captured and imprisoned at Carrick House, before being transferred to London for execution.

considered this an auspicious site, choosing it for several burials.

Make sure to check out the small but informative museum, which explains what brochs are, displays a selection of archeological finds from the site, and gives an insight into the people who once lived here.

Fernvalley Wildlife Centre

MAP PAGE 34
Tingwall, KW17 2HB
Ⓦ fernvalleywildlifecentre.co.uk.
April–Sept Thurs–Mon 10am–4pm; Oct–March Fri–Sun 10am–4pm. Charge.
Fernvalley Wildlife Centre is mostly home to animals that were victims of the exotic pet trade, who were rescued from unsuitable homes or simply abandoned to their fate. In the well-designed centre, you'll have the chance to see snakes, lemurs and raccoon dogs, among smaller animals such as axolotls, parakeets and hedgehog tenrecs. The lemurs and raccoon dogs can also access outdoor enclosures, and you'll find meerkats outside too. There are excellent information boards throughout, giving both an insight into the different species and the life stories of the individual animals. Elsewhere on site, there's a tearoom (with a great view of both the sea and the lemur enclosure) serving very good cakes, a small maze, and – a little incongruously – a short display on the eighteenth-century pirate John Gow (see box, page 39).

Rendall Doocot

MAP PAGE 34
Rendall, KW17 2EZ. Open 24hr. Free.
Dating back to the seventeenth century, this dome-shaped stone structure was a home for the pigeons belonging to the nearby landowners. **Rendall Doocot** is perhaps not worth a special trip, but if you're needing a diversion to kill time while waiting for a ferry at Tingwall, it could be just the ticket.

Wideford Hill Chambered Cairn

MAP PAGE 34
Off Old Finstown Rd, KW15 1TR
Ⓦ historicenvironment.scot/visit-a-place/places/wideford-hill-chambered-cairn.
Open 24hr. Free.
Among all the archeological sites on Orkney, **Wideford Hill Chambered Cairn** is perhaps the one that makes you feel most like an archeologist yourself. This is because you enter from the top, sliding open a trapdoor and climbing down a ladder into the cool darkness beneath; it's easy to imagine yourself an Indiana Jones in these circumstances. The attractively round cairn was built more than five thousand years ago, likely with now long-forgotten ritualistic significance concerning the interment of the dead. It was happened upon by chance in the early 1800s and has been excavated at least twice subsequently, but no remains have been discovered within: it's thought that at some point in the

The Orkneyinga Saga

Written in Iceland in Old Norse in the late twelfth century, the Orkneyinga Saga (meaning "Saga of the Orkney Men") relates the lives and deeds of the Norse Earls of Orkney, with particular emphasis on especially exciting incidents. It's one of our main sources of information on important events such as the martyrdom of St Magnus, the antics of a Viking named Swein Asliefarson, and the reign of Earl Thorfinn. The Saga was, however, written as entertainment rather than history, and it cannot be relied upon to be entirely true.

distant past, the cairn was emptied and blocked up. Views from the cairn are stunning; there's an obvious path, sometimes paved, running to it from a car park near the summit of the hill.

Cuween Hill

MAP PAGE 34
Old Finstown Rd, KW17 2EJ
ⓦ historicenvironment.scot/visit-a-place/places/cuween-hill-chambered-cairn.
Open 24hr. Free.

At the top of **Cuween Hill**, just outside Finstown, is an ancient chambered cairn that, when excavated, was found to contain the remains of eight people and the skulls of twenty-four dogs, the latter thought to be of ritualistic importance. You can enter the cairn to explore, but the passage has an extremely low ceiling, and it's not recommended if you're at all claustrophobic. Once you get inside, there's space to stand up. It's a five- to ten-minute easy walk up from the car park on the side of the hill.

A little further up, there's what appears to be a stone circle from a distance, but get up close and you'll see the standing stones are in fact newer cairns made by more recent visitors. There are fabulous views into the Bay of Firth from this vantage point.

Orkneyinga Saga Centre

MAP PAGE 34
1 Gyre Rd, Orphir, KW17 2RD.
Daily 9am–6pm. Free.

A small but engaging exhibition introduces you to the world of the sagas, with obvious particular emphasis on the Orkneyinga Saga (see box, page 40). You'll learn what a saga is, who the main characters of the Orkneyinga Saga were, and – perhaps most usefully – about Viking drinking etiquette. A fifteen-minute film plays at the press of a button, in which the most exciting segments of the saga are related.

Rendall Doocot

Behind the **Orkneyinga Saga Centre**, a short path leads to a round church thought to have been built in the twelfth century, possibly inspired by the Holy Sepulchre in Jerusalem. It's one of only two round churches in Scotland, the other being at Roxburgh, south of Edinburgh. Here, you'll also find the scanty remains of the Bu of Orphir, a drinking hall believed to be the scene of one of the Orkneyinga Saga's most dramatic moments, a drunken brawl between two chaps called Swein.

If you're in the mood for a relaxed coastal amble, a path wends from the church's graveyard down to a pebbly beach and along the shoreline.

East of Orphir

MAP PAGE 34

From Orphir, the A964 road heads east to Kirkwall, taking in a couple of worthwhile stops en route. First up is Waulkmill Bay, an attractive sandy beach which is a haven for birdlife. A little distance further on is Hobbister Hill, a nature reserve offering another excellent birdwatching spot, as well as pleasant moorland walks.

Shops

Castaway Crafts

MAP PAGE 34
A986, Dounby, KW17 2HT
Ⓦ castawaycrafts.co.uk.
Mon–Fri 10am–4pm, Sat 11am–3pm.
Castaway Crafts is owned by
designer Fiona Mitchell, whose
fine range of Orkney tweed is on
sale here, alongside products made
by local craftspeople, including
artwork, knitwear, jewellery and
much more besides.

Harray Potter

MAP PAGE 34
A986, Harray, KW17 2JR
Ⓦ orkneypottery.co.uk.
Mon–Fri 9.48am–5.51pm,
Sun 12.47pm–5.58pm (yes, really).
Well, if you live in Harray
and you make pottery, you're
definitely going to call your shop
Harray Potter, aren't you? Having
been making pottery since he
was a child, the friendly Andrew
Appleby produces beautiful
works, ranging from plates and
cups to teapots and vases, all
available in a variety of colours.

Andrew Appleby at Harray Potter

It's an excellent place to find a
unique Orkney souvenir.

Yellowbird Gallery

MAP PAGE 34
A966, Birsay, KW17 2LT
Ⓦ yellowbirdgallery.scot.
No set hours, but usually 9am–6pm.
Beautiful and slightly abstract
artwork, with a strong emphasis
on puffins, is the order of the day
at this small gallery near Birsay.
Original works will make quite an
indent on your wallet, but there
are prints and cards available too,
which are much more affordable.
If you're heading on to the
Brough of Birsay, check out the
helpful tidal clock here first to
ensure you'll be able to cross
the causeway.

Restaurants

The Foveran

MAP PAGE 34
Off A964, Kirkwall, KW15 1SF
Ⓦ thefoveran.com.
Mon–Sat 6–8pm.
A lovely upmarket restaurant
with views over Scapa Flow,
The Foveran is a great choice to
mark a special occasion. The
menu, most of it locally sourced,
includes such delights as pan-
fried Orkney scallops and fillet
steak topped with haggis and
whisky cream sauce; if you've
still got room, the desserts are
equally delicious. ££££

The Merkister

MAP PAGE 34
Russland Rd, Harray, KW17 2LF
Ⓦ merkister.com/restaurant.
Daily 5.30–8.30pm.
A stunning lochside location is
the calling card for the *Merkister
Hotel*: on a sunny evening, the
view from the dining room is
gorgeous. Fortunately, the food
measures up to the vistas: alongside
the excellent choices on the regular
menu, there's an ever-changing and

lengthy list of specials. The Orkney beef and ale pie is particularly recommended. £££

Standing Stones Hotel

MAP PAGE 34
A965, Stromness, KW16 3JX
Ⓦ thestandingstones.co.uk/food.
Daily 6.30–8.30pm.

The restaurant of the *Standing Stones Hotel* is a good place for unfussy, filling main meals: Orkney steak-and-ale pie and fish and chips are both tasty choices, and there are some good dessert options on the menu too. The restaurant could perhaps do with a little more atmosphere, but since the food's good, that perhaps doesn't matter. £££

The Foveran

Cafés

Eviedale Bakehouse & Bistro

MAP PAGE 34
A966, Evie, KW17 2PJ
Ⓦ eviedale-cottages.co.uk/bistro.
Fri & Sat 5–7.30pm.

Operating only as a pre-order takeaway at time of research, *Eviedale Bakehouse & Bistro* offers a tantalizing selection of bakery products, though where it really excels is in its wood-fired sourdough pizzas. Visit on a sunny evening, select from an extensive menu – the Neopolitana with anchovies, capers and olives is a strong choice, as is the tongue-tingling hot chilli Hawaiian – and enjoy it on the nearby Evie beach. Perfect. ££

The Waterside

MAP PAGE 34
A965, Finstown, KW17 2EH Ⓦ facebook.
com/beitingandbrewatthewaterside.
Mon–Sat 8.30am–4pm.

The views over the bay from this laidback café are great, as is the food. There's a good breakfast menu, but lunch is even better, with a diverse array of international options such as American bagels, Korean barbecue and Szechuan dan dan noodles. The Orkney crab rarebit is a particularly solid choice. It's conveniently located if you're looking for a place to pick up a takeaway lunch to munch on as you explore Mainland. ££

Pub

Smithfield Hotel

MAP PAGE 34
A986, Dounby, KW17 2HT
Ⓦ smithfieldhotel.co.uk/index.php/
restaurant. Daily 5–8pm.

A great range of menu choices, offering plenty of local produce – try the crab linguine, for example, or the excellent Westray scallops. For meat-eaters, there's Orkney beef and a good selection of burgers, while vegetarians are catered for with a lovely macaroni cheese, among other choices. Much of the menu can be made gluten-free, too. There are some great desserts on offer – if you have room, the sticky toffee pudding is really very good. £££

Hoy, South Walls and Flotta

Hoy, South Walls and Flotta – the ensemble of islands south of Stromness and on the west side of Scapa Flow – have perhaps Orkney's greatest concentration of wartime heritage, including the Hackness Martello Tower and Battery on South Walls, Scapa Flow Museum at Hoy's Lyness, and Stanger Battery on Flotta. That's not all these islands have to offer, though: Hoy boasts one of Orkney's most iconic destinations, the tremendous sea stack known as the Old Man of Hoy, and it's also home to a second excellent museum, while South Walls will delight with its soul-stirring coastal walks. Flotta is one of Orkney's least-visited islands, but if you make the effort, you'll be rewarded with a beautiful coastline and a small but very good heritage centre.

Hoy

As the home of the Old Man of Hoy, one of Orkney's best-known sights, Hoy is a popular destination for visitors keen to explore Orkney's most rugged coastline. Much of the island is uninhabited, with just a smattering of small settlements, concentrated largely along the east coast. Besides the Old Man, the island offers two brilliant museums, a distinctive prehistoric tomb, and plenty of hiking opportunities, including the 479m-tall Ward Hill, Orkney's highest point.

Hoy Kirk Heritage Centre

MAP PAGE 46
B9047, Hoy, KW16 3NJ. Ⓦ hoyheritage. wordpress.com. Open 24hr. Free.
Housed in the old Hoy church, the **Hoy Kirk Heritage Centre** contains displays on a variety of Hoy-focused themes, including shipwrecks, the neolithic Dwarfie Stane tomb, and, of course, the Old Man of Hoy, of which there are some great old photos and newspaper clippings detailing bold attempts to summit the sea stack. You'll find exhibits on local luminaries such as James Sinclair, a keen botanist, and William Ritch, who was born and died in Hoy but worked for the Hudson Bay Company in Canada for thirty-eight years. There is also a small library of local-interest titles, making it a great resource for those researching Hoy in depth. Much of the church's original furniture has been removed to make room for the exhibitions, but the pulpit – thought to have been carved from the wood of a Spanish Armada wreck – remains, as does

Reaching Hoy

Car ferries to Hoy depart from Houton, near Orphir, up to six times a day, and take thirty-five minutes to sail to Lyness. Foot passengers can hop on the ferry from Stromness, which takes thirty minutes to reach Moaness; some of these ferries sail via Graemsay, so it's possible to stop off at this small island en route and visit its two lighthouses and minor church ruins.

a cross made from the wreckage of HMS *Vanguard*, which suffered an internal explosion and sank in Scapa Flow in 1917.

Moaness beaches

MAP PAGE 46
You'll find attractive **beaches** unfurling either side of the Moaness Pier – to the north, the Sands of Klebreck offers a fine sandy outlook across the bay, while to the south, the Bay of Quoys is a little less accessible but decent enough for rockpooling.

Braebister Mound

MAP PAGE 46
Braebister – an earth mound that is possibly a broch – is perhaps not the most exciting of Orkney's prehistoric monuments, but it's still worth the 45-minute out-and-back walk for the rugged scenery alone. Leave your car before the cattle grid, walk down the lane and past the cottages, then take the right-hand gate towards the sea, heading down through a field and over a stile. To the left of the mound, the sea stack of Ber Log presents some pretty funky geology,

and in the distance you'll see an arch in the headland beyond. To the mound's right, there's a small but impressive chasm into which the sea crashes alarmingly. Head back the same way.

Ward Hill

MAP PAGE 46
The tallest point on Orkney, at 479m, the brooding mass of Ward Hill is possible to climb, but it's not a proposition to be undertaken lightly. There's no specific path up, and it's therefore quite tough-going over often-boggy land. The best route is from the south side, where the hill isn't quite so steep. At the summit, the views are stunning, offering splendid panoramas across the whole archipelago.

Dwarfie Stane

MAP PAGE 46
Road to Rackwick, Hoy, KW16 3NJ
ⓦ historicenvironment.scot/visit-a-place/ places/dwarfie-stane. Open 24hr. Free.
Folklore, particularly Walter Scott's novel *The Pirate*, has it that this ancient burial chamber was the home of dwarfs and trolls, for reasons which become obvious

Dwarfie Stane

46

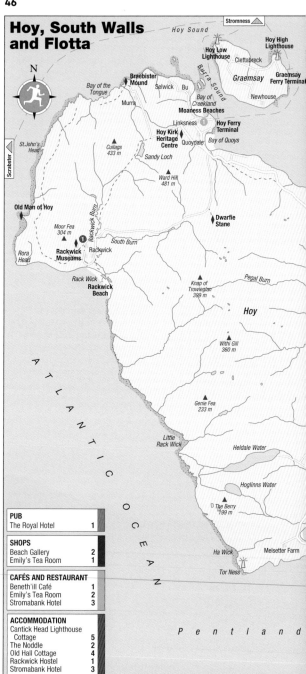

Hoy, South Walls and Flotta

HOY, SOUTH WALLS AND FLOTTA

PUB
The Royal Hotel | 1

SHOPS
Beach Gallery | 2
Emily's Tea Room | 1

CAFÉS AND RESTAURANT
Beneth'ill Café | 1
Emily's Tea Room | 2
Stromabank Hotel | 3

ACCOMMODATION
Cantick Head Lighthouse Cottage | 5
The Noddle | 2
Old Hall Cottage | 4
Rackwick Hostel | 1
Stromabank Hotel | 3

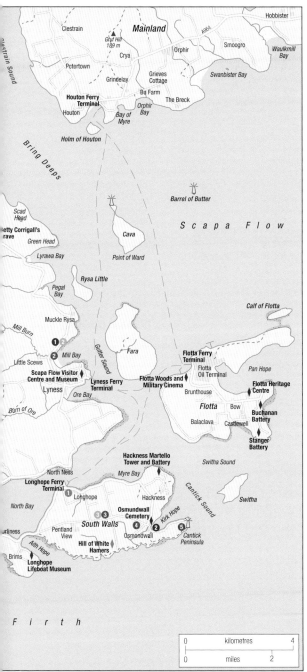

when you enter: it's extremely small, even by the standards of such tombs. The **Dwarfie Stane** was hollowed out from a large sandstone block, making it possibly Britain's only rock-hewn tomb. The exterior is etched with historic graffiti, including an inscription scored in Persian by William Mounsey, a nineteenth-century army officer who seems to have had a habit of making carvings in prehistoric remains through Britain. A boardwalk path from the small car park leads up to it, allowing easy access even when the ground is wet.

Rackwick museums

MAP PAGE 46

Rackwick, Hoy, KW16 3NJ. Open 24hr. Free.

The village of Rackwick, best known as the start point for the walk to the Old Man of Hoy, is home to a trio of small **museums**, dotting the hillside above the village. The first that you come to – the **School House** – gives a short and reasonably engaging history of education in Rackwick, including the interesting titbit that eighteenth-century schoolchildren paid for their attendance with a piece of peat every day. Outside, you'll find a selection of rusting farm machinery, which is unlikely to divert you for long.

Opposite the School House is **Glen House**, labelled on the door as 'Archive Centre'. One room here contains a small display on the scuttling of the German fleet in Scapa Flow in 1919, while the other is set up as a typical Rackwick home of the early 1900s. If you're on Hoy to research your family history, there are also copies of nineteenth-century census records here.

A little further along, leave the path and head up through a field to your right to visit the turf-roofed **Craa Nest**, the best of Rackwick's three museums. This eighteenth-century house is laid out with ethnographic exhibits, giving a truly evocative impression of life here in days gone by. Look out in particular for the amazing box beds. Rather incongruously, there's also a small display on the history of suspender belts, which were apparently invented by a former inhabitant of this house.

Old Man of Hoy

MAP PAGE 46

Orkney's most iconic natural sight, the **Old Man of Hoy** is a dramatic sea stack. Towering 137 metres above the ocean's surface, it's a powerful reminder of the awesome force of the sea: the stack is all that remains of a headland that once jutted out from this spot, but at some point between 1750 and 1819, the land collapsed, leaving the Old Man standing

Walking from Rackwick to the Old Man of Hoy

From Rackwick's car park, take the road signposted to the Old Man, albeit with a rather faded sign. This leads you directly to the cliff path, involving a short but steep ascent. For a gentler climb, consider taking the path from the car park, which will take you to the cliff trail via the trio of museums. Follow the waymarkers illustrated with a seabird, then take the obvious route along the top of the cliffs. The path initially hugs the cliff edge – take care, as these are sheer drops – then after a while, cuts inland across the headland. You'll soon see your destination ahead. Allow two to three hours for the out-and-back walk.

The Longhope lifeboat disaster

The Longhope lifeboat station experienced tragedy in March 1969, when the lifeboat *T.G.B.* answered a call for help from the Liberian vessel *Irene*. Launching in a force nine gale at 8pm, the *T.G.B.* was last heard from at 9.28pm, and the following day was found capsized. All eight lifeboat men lost their lives, devastating the community: it's particularly hard to imagine the grief felt by the two families who each lost three people. The disaster met with an outpouring of sympathy from across the entire country, with a radio appeal by the broadcaster Raymond Baxter resulting in financial aid for the affected families. Astonishingly, many among the small community volunteered to form a new lifeboat crew, demonstrating a remarkable heroism. There's a memorial to the disaster at the Osmundwall Cemetery on South Walls, and an enormously moving display in the Longhope Lifeboat Museum.

alone in the water. First climbed in 1966 by Chris Bonington, Rusty Baillie and Tom Patey, it's no mean feat. Fortunately, you won't need to ascend its flanks to get a good look at it: there's a well-maintained trail from Rackwick to an excellent viewpoint.

Betty Corrigall's Grave

MAP PAGE 46

B9047, Hoy, KW16 3NU. Open 24hr. Free.

By the side of the pretty lake known as the Water of Hoy, a short boardwalk leads to **Betty Corrigall's Grave**. In the 1770s, Betty was twenty-seven years old, unmarried and pregnant, with the father of her child having run away to sea. Faced with condemnation from her local community, Betty hanged herself, and as she died by suicide, she was denied burial on consecrated ground. Instead, she was laid to rest in an unmarked grave, which was then rediscovered in the 1930s, her body preserved by the peat. She was eventually reburied at this site, with a fibreglass headstone erected in 1976.

On the other side of the road, there's a track leading up to Lyrawa Hill, which offers fine views across Scapa Flow as well as to a World War II anti-aircraft defence battery.

Scapa Flow Visitor Centre and Museum

MAP PAGE 46

Lyness, Hoy, KW16 3NT

🛈 01856 791300, 🌐 orkney.gov.uk/Service-Directory/S/scapa-flow-museum. May–Sept daily 9.30am–4.15pm; Oct–Dec Tues–Sat 9.30am–4.15pm; March Thurs–Sat 9.30am–4.15pm; April Mon–Sat 9.30am–4.15pm. Free.

Pretty much the first thing you'll see when you disembark from the ferry at Lyness is the **Scapa Flow**

Old Man of Hoy

Longhope Lifeboat Museum

head up there for great views over Scapa Flow. Interestingly, the hill is hollow, having been dug out during the 1940s in order to house vast quantities of oil containers.

Longhope Lifeboat Museum

MAP PAGE 46
Off B9047, Hoy, KW16 3NZ
ⓦ longhopelifeboat.org.uk/museum.
Wed–Fri 11am–4pm. Free.

Longhope's former lifeboat station sits at the very bottom of Hoy, just before the road crosses a small causeway to Longhope town on South Walls. It has been lovingly converted into a fascinating **museum**, with pride of place going to the historic Longhope lifeboat *Thomas McCunn* itself, poised on its slipway and occasionally launched for special occasions. You can walk on the boat to examine it at close quarters: it's had a long and eventful history, from its launch in 1933 to a period spent as a private boat in the late twentieth century before its return to Orkney in 2001. Make sure to chat to Mike, who's here during opening hours and can share a wealth of knowledge about the history of the local lifeboat service and of Hoy in general. The museum is also home to plenty of lifeboat memorabilia and contains a special display on the disaster of 1969 (see box, page 49).

South Walls

Connected to Hoy by a causeway, South Walls is a small island that's blessed with gorgeous coastal scenery, particularly in the

Visitor Centre and Museum, which reopened in July 2022 after several years of renovation. The new museum is a state-of-the-art affair, including virtual-reality displays and interactive exhibits, many of which have been specifically designed to engage children. Thanks to the renovations, the museum now boasts significantly improved environmental conditions, making it possible for a considerable number of previously unseen artefacts to be shown.

   Lyness itself is home to a considerable number of World War II remains, not many of which are particularly interesting if you're not an avid military historian. The most rewarding, perhaps, is **Wee Fea**, the concrete Naval Signal Station that's pokes above the hill just beyond Lyness;

Reaching South Walls

If you're already on Hoy, you can reach South Walls by driving across the causeway at Hoy's southern end, near the Lifeboat Museum. Alternatively, there are daily ferries from Houton to Longhope, which sail via Lyness and Flotta and take 1hr 20min.

Sigurd Hlodvisson

Sigurd Hlodvisson, also known as Sigurd the Stout, was the Norse Earl of Orkney between 991 and 1014. According to the Orkneyinga Saga, one of the principal sources for our knowledge of Hlodvisson, he rather sagely converted on South Walls in 995 when the Norwegian King Olaf Tryggvasson popped by to inform him that if he didn't adopt Christianity, he'd be instantly killed and his dominions ravaged. The saga suggests that following this incident, Orkney became Christian immediately but, in actual fact, it's likely that Christianity was prevalent here for some time prior to Sigurd's era.

southeast corner. You'll also find historical sites here, including the Hackness Martello Tower and Battery and the memorial to the Longhope lifeboat disaster in Osmundwall Cemetery. The island's main settlement is Longhope, which is not a particularly large place but does boast a pub and a small shop.

Hackness Martello Tower and Battery

MAP PAGE 46
Hackness, South Walls, KW16 3PQ
Ⓦ historicenvironment.scot/visit-a-place/places/hackness-martello-tower-and-battery. Daily April–Sept, by guided tour only 10.15am, noon & 2.30pm. Charge.
Built for Britain's 1812 war against the United States, the pair of towers at the mouth of the Longhope Sound spent over a century defending this strategic stretch of water before eventually being sold into private ownership in 1922. The tower on Hoy remains inaccessible to the public, but the **Hackness Martello Tower and Battery** on South Walls is now a museum run by Historic Scotland. Visits are by guided tour only, lasting approximately one hour and delivered by the genuinely enthusiastic curator. The highlight, perhaps, is the room depicting the family history of John Cload, who lived here from 1922 until his death in 2020, including some fascinating

memorabilia of his exploits in World War II.

Osmundwall Cemetery

MAP PAGE 46
B9047, South Walls, KW16 3PQ.
Open 24hr. Free.
At South Walls' eastern end, the central feature of the well-maintained **Osmundwall Cemetery** is a tribute to those who tragically lost their lives in the Longhope lifeboat disaster of 1969. The memorial consists of a statue of a lifeboatman, gazing out to sea, surrounded by the graves of the fallen. Just outside the graveyard

Hackness Martello Tower

Reaching Flotta

Flotta is served by up to four ferries daily from Houton, which take between thirty-five minutes and one hour, depending on whether the boat is calling at Lyness first. There are also three ferries daily from Lyness, taking fifteen minutes.

is a bench bedecked with stone carvings that tell the story of the conversion of the Earl of Orkney, Sigurd Hlodvisson (see box, page 51), to Christianity.

Cantick Peninsula

MAP PAGE 46

A lovely sixty- to ninety-minute walk starts from the car park just south of the Osmundwall Cemetery. The path leads out of the car park to the south of the **Cantick Peninsula**; once you reach the sea, turn left and follow the trail along the gorgeous headland. The walk takes you past beautiful stacked rocks and several mildly diverting archeological sites, including the grassy Hesti Geo Broch and the Roeberry Barrow, before reaching the **Cantick Head Lighthouse**. Here,

South Walls coastline

you may have to limbo under the fence to pick up the path on the other side, which takes you down to a small road. Follow this to the left around the attractive bay, bringing you back to the car park.

Hill of White Hamers

MAP PAGE 46
South Walls, KW16 3PQ
Ⓦ scottishwildlifetrust.org.uk/reserve/hill-of-white-hamars. Open 24hr. Free.
A bumpy track leads to a small parking area at the access point to the **Hill of White Hamers**, a nature reserve maintained by the Scottish Wildlife Trust. If truth be told, there's no hill here, with white hamers or without, but it is a lovely stretch of coastline, sculpted by picturesque inlets and rocky outcrops, making it perfect for walks of various lengths. If you head left from the parking area, you can reach the Hesti Geo Broch and connect with the walk to the lighthouse.

Flotta

The small island of **Flotta**, to Hoy's east, is best known for its large oil terminal, which was opened in 1977 and still processes approximately ten percent of the UK's oil. Visitors to the island will perhaps be more interested in Flotta's extensive wartime remains and its excellent little heritage centre.

Flotta Heritage Centre

MAP PAGE 46
Flotta, KW16 3NP. Daily 10am–6pm. Free.
The **Flotta Heritage Centre** consists of a small cottage, decorated as it might have looked

Buchanan Battery

in the 1940s – a living room with a fine stove, a bedroom with an open box bed, and a smaller room containing a record player and other period artefacts. Don't miss flipping through the 1930s book giving thoughts, household hints and a recipe for each day of the year.

Next door, in the barn, you'll find a remarkable treasure trove of information about life on Flotta, with well-presented exhibits, information boards and photos detailing the various ways the islanders have found employment over the centuries, including farming, fishing, peat-cutting, and working at the oil refinery. Highlights of the exhibition include World War II memorabilia, a 1954 issue of iconic comic magazine *The Beano*, and a rather disconcerting Esso tiger mascot. Surprisingly for an island as small and infrequently visited as Flotta, this is one of the best heritage centres in Orkney.

Flotta World War II sites

MAP PAGE 46

The southeast coast of Flotta rewards military historians with an abundance of abandoned concrete remains from the war. The most easily accessible site is **Buchanan Battery**, which is only a short walk from the road – you can park at the information board and wander round the slightly eerie empty site.

In the southeast corner, the more substantial **Stanger Battery** stands in a beautiful spot, its starkly functional concrete lines contrasting sharply with the surrounding vistas. From Stanger, you can also see a pair of impressive sea stacks, known locally as the **Cletts**. Access to the Stanger Battery is down a rough but driveable track.

Beyond these, perhaps the most interesting and curious World War II remains on Flotta can be found just south of the ferry terminal, where a small woodland was planted by the bored ratings who were stationed here during the war years.

Here, too, are the ruins of the military cinema, which is now derelict but was once among the most popular entertainment spots on the island.

Shops

Beach Gallery

MAP PAGE 46

Cantick Rd, Longhope, South Walls, KW16 3PQ ☎ 01307 724904, ⓦ beachgallery.co.uk. Fri–Sun 11am–4pm.

A lovely place found close to the Osmundwall Cemetery, the *Beach Gallery* sells a fantastic selection of artwork and pottery, but it's the beautiful hand-painted glass baubles that really set it apart from the crowd. There's also a good tearoom here, too, serving up excellent coffee and freshly baked cake.

Emily's Tea Room

MAP PAGE 46

Lyness, Hoy, KW16 3NU ☎ 01856 791213, ⓦ emilystearoomhoy. co.uk. Mon–Sat 10am–5pm.

Attached to the café of the same name (see opposite), there's a small craft shop selling locally made items such as glass coasters, knitwear, jewellery, notelets and much else besides. It's a great place to pick up an individual souvenir of your trip.

Emily's Tea Room

Restaurant

Stromabank Hotel

MAP PAGE 46

Longhope, South Walls, KW16 3PA ☎ 01856 701494, ⓦ stromabank.co.uk. Daily 6–8.30pm.

The dining room of the *Stromabank Hotel* has fantastic panoramic views, stretching from Orkney's east Mainland all the way to Cape Wrath and Dunnet Head. The small menu features various pub classics, including scampi, pork loin, and a good range of burgers. The desserts are good too. ££

Cafés

Beneth'ill Café

MAP PAGE 46

Moaness, Hoy, KW16 3NJ ☎ 01856 791119, ⓦ benethillcafe.co.uk. Daily 10am–6pm.

With a fine location beneath the looming presence of Ward Hill, overlooking the Sands of Klebreck and offering views across to Graemsay, this café is ahead of the game from the start. The food and

Picnic on Hoy

drink measures up: there's a wide range of sandwiches, salads and paninis, as well as specials that may include local scallops or Hungarian goulash. The large selection of local beers makes it perfect, especially if you're here on a warm sunny day and can enjoy them in the garden. £

Emily's Tea Room

MAP PAGE 46

Lyness, Hoy, KW16 3NU ☎ 01856 791213, ⓦ emilystearoomhoy.co.uk. Mon–Wed 10am–5pm, Thurs–Sat 10am–8pm.

A lovely little café overlooking an inlet of Scapa Flow, *Emily's Tea Room* serves up a tempting selection of cakes and ice creams, as well as more substantial fare at breakfast and lunchtime. The waffle with bacon and maple syrup is a decadent treat. On Thurs, Fri and Sat, the tearoom is also open for evening meals, with a focus on local fish and seafood – it's worth booking ahead. Also note that it's close to the ferry port at Lyness, so is often very busy in the lunchtime hour before the ferry departs. ££

Pub

The Royal Hotel

MAP PAGE 46

Manse Rd, Longhope, South Walls, KW16 3PG ☎ 01856 701276. Daily 6–8.30pm.

Fish and chips is the speciality here, and they're extremely good. Coupled with a fine selection of beers and whiskies, and a friendly welcoming atmosphere, it's no wonder *The Royal Hotel* is so popular – so ignore everything else on the menu and get stuck in. ££

Eating on Flotta

There are no restaurants or cafés on Flotta, though you can pick up supplies from the island shop, near the heritage centre. You may wish to bring food with you, in case the shop is closed.

Kirkwall

Orkney's capital is a small but buzzing and cosmopolitan place, where you'll find the islands' widest selection of shops, cafés and restaurants, as well as a cluster of important historical attractions. Foremost of these is the UK's northernmost cathedral, dedicated to St Magnus and built of gorgeous red and yellow sandstone. Across the street is the Orkney Museum, an excellent exhibition boasting remarkable finds from sites across the islands. Consider also setting aside some time to explore the Mainland to Kirkwall's east too: this often-neglected corner of Orkney offers some fine coastal walking.

St Magnus Cathedral

MAP PAGE 58
Broad St, Kirkwall, KW15 1NX Ⓦ stmagnus.
org. Mon–Sat 9am–5pm, Sun 1–5pm. Free.
A distinctive structure that can be seen from all over town, **St Magnus Cathedral** is dedicated to the Earl of Orkney (see box, page 57), who was martyred in the early twelfth century. Construction on the church began in 1137 and continued for some three hundred years. It was worth the wait though:

St Magnus Cathedral

the beautiful facade conceals an interior that is simply stunning – the red sandstone pillars and arched walls give it a unique style and atmosphere that you'll find in no other cathedral in Britain. Elaborately carved gravestones, mostly from the seventeenth century, line the walls – the oldest, thought to date back to the 1200s, can be found in the chapel, where you'll also see intricate carvings on the pillars. Keep an eye out, too, for the memorial to those lost on the HMS *Royal Oak* in 1939, as well as the creepy Mort Brod hanging from a pillar, depicting Death carrying an hourglass and a spade.

Tours of the cathedral's upper levels, offering fantastic views over Kirkwall and the interior of the cathedral, run twice a day on Tuesdays, Thursdays and Sundays between April and September, and on Thursdays and Saturdays between October and March. The tours (charge) must be prebooked by calling Ⓣ 01856 874894.

Orkney Museum

MAP PAGE 58
Broad St, Kirkwall, KW15 1DH Ⓣ 01856 873191. Mon–Sat 10.30am–5pm. Free.
The **Orkney Museum**, with its series of extensive and well-presented galleries, takes you

St Magnus

Magnus was an Earl of Orkney in the early twelfth century, who was described in the Orkneyinga Saga as "a most excellent man". The Saga then goes on to list Magnus' many virtues, which apparently included his habit of bathing in cold water if ever tempted by carnal lusts. Whether this is true or not, it is certain that the position of Earl of Orkney was disputed between Magnus and his cousin Hákon. An agreement was reached that they would share the title between them, but in around 1117, Hákon took Magnus prisoner on the island of Egilsay. Prompted by his men, Hákon then had Magnus executed and became the sole Earl.

Magnus was buried in Birsay, on the site where St Magnus Church now stands, and his burial place was soon associated with miracles, most commonly the curing of illnesses. Although the Bishop of Orkney remained unconvinced for some time, he was eventually persuaded of Magnus' sanctity, and arranged for Magnus to be canonized in 1135. Magnus' remains were transferred to St Magnus Cathedral around 1137.

through the history of the archipelago, starting with a surprisingly interesting section on the islands' chair-making traditions. It's difficult to choose a highlight from the museum, but Orkney's many neolithic sites, the Iron Age and the medieval period are all well represented with an excellent collection of artefacts. You should also make sure not to miss the Pictish section with its remarkable exhibition of carved symbol stones, among plenty of artefacts detailing everyday life for the Picts.

The Viking gallery contains a very fine collection of items, including a beautifully carved whalebone plaque adorned with mythical creatures. Elsewhere, the nineteenth- and twentieth-century galleries have a wealth of artefacts and fascinating facts – we learn, for example, that for the first half of the twentieth century, Orkney was at the forefront of the British egg industry – as well as a fairly extensive collection of World War II exhibits.

There are a couple of interactive activities for children, including a brilliant 'design your own medieval Kirkwall', which allows kids to consider the advantages and disadvantages of placing various industries in town – would you put the smelly tannery right next to the cathedral, for example?

Tankerness Gardens

MAP PAGE 58
Tankerness Ln, Kirkwall, KW15 1GY.
Open 24hr. Free.

Behind the museum, the **Tankerness Gardens** contain a small lawn, some attractive enough flowerbeds, and a rather haphazard rockery. The main point of interest is the Grootie Hoose, a conical structure built using ballast stones from the *Revenge*, the ship of the infamous pirate John Gow.

Earl's Palace

MAP PAGE 58
Watergate, Kirkwall, KW15 1PD
ⓦ historicenvironment.scot/visit-a-place/
places/bishop-s-and-earl-s-palaces-
kirkwall. April–Sept Sun–Thurs 9.30am–
noon & 1–5.30pm, Sat 10am–noon &
1–5pm. Charge.

Built in the early 1600s for the notoriously unpleasant Earl Patrick Stewart (see box, above),

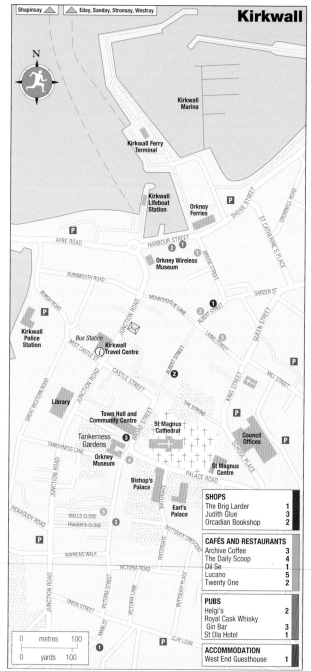

Kirkwall

Shapinsay

Eday, Sanday, Stronsay, Westray

SHOPS

The Brig Larder	1
Judith Glue	3
Orcadian Bookshop	2

CAFÉS AND RESTAURANTS

Archive Coffee	3
The Daily Scoop	4
Dil Se	1
Lucano	5
Twenty One	2

PUBS

Helgi's	2
Royal Cask Whisky Gin Bar	3
St Ola Hotel	1

ACCOMMODATION

West End Guesthouse	1

Earl Patrick

Patrick Stewart, the Earl of Orkney from 1593 until 1615, was an illegitimate cousin of King James VI, and although the two were friends in their youth, the relationship soured once Patrick succeeded to the earldom. His rule was characterized by arrogance, cruelty and financial irresponsibility, and his various extravagant enterprises left him deep in debt. Ordered to hand over his newly completed Earl's Palace to the Bishop of Orkney in 1607, he did not make it so until 1610, by which time he had been imprisoned in Edinburgh Castle as a result of the islanders' complaints against his tyrannical rule. Apparently unable to accept the inevitable, he worsened his situation by ordering his son Robert to engage in rebellion against the crown, with the result that both he and Robert were executed for treason in 1615. Legend has it that Patrick's execution was delayed for several days to allow him time to learn the Lord's Prayer, as he was so evil-hearted that he did not know it.

the **Earl's Palace** was designed to impress, with an attractive facade punctuated by built-out windows; an enormous kitchen suggesting lavish entertainment; and a huge Great Hall in which feasts were held. Though it's fallen into ruin somewhat, the remains are substantial and reward exploration.

Bishop's Palace

MAP PAGE 58

Watergate, Kirkwall, KW15 1PD
Ⓦ historicenvironment.scot/visit-a-place/places/bishop-s-and-earl-s-palaces-kirkwall. April–Sept Sun–Thurs 9.30am–noon & 1–5.30pm, Sat 10am–noon & 1–5pm. Charge.

Across the road from the Earl's Palace, and included on the same ticket, this older palace was the home of Orkney's medieval bishops. There's less to see than in the Earl's Palace, and one of the most impressive features – the enormous ice cream cone-shaped carving which would have once been beneath an upper floor window – is on the exterior anyway.

Still, the **Bishop's Palace** ruins offer an evocative view of St Magnus Cathedral from the spot on your right immediately after

you enter, and they are worth a quick nose about.

Orkney Wireless Museum

MAP PAGE 58

1 Junction Rd, Kirkwall, KW15 1LB
Ⓦ gb2owm.org.uk. Mon & Thurs–Sat 10.30am–1pm & 1.30–4pm, Wed 10.30am–1pm. Free.

Radio history enthusiasts will be in seventh heaven in the dinky

Grootie Hoose, Tankerness Gardens

Orkney Wireless Museum, which is home to a vast quantity of antique wireless sets, stretching back from the very first days of radio into the 1950s and beyond. There is also a number of other intriguing pieces from Orkney's technological history, including a fabulous jukebox that was the first on the islands, and a set of 'his and hers' headphones for use in church. It's entirely run by volunteers, and opening hours are not set in stone.

Highland Park Whisky Distillery

MAP PAGE 60
Holm Rd, KW15 1SU
ⓦ highlandparkwhisky.com/en/distillery.
April–Oct daily 10am–5pm; Nov–March Tues–Sat 10am–5pm, by tour only. Charge.

Highland Park produces several of Orkney's finest whiskies, and also offers the chance to explore the distillery and learn about how they are made – and, of course, try

a few. Four different levels of tour are available, depending on the number and quality of whiskies you want to sample. You'll need to book your visit in advance, and do remember that Scotland's drink-driving laws are stricter than those in the rest of the UK: it's much wiser to reach **Highland Park Whisky Distillery** by public transport.

East of Kirkwall

The Mainland east of Kirkwall isn't home to any of Orkney's big-hitters, but it's definitely worth visiting regardless. Here, you'll find a string of lovely beaches, a couple of low-key historical sites, and a great cliff walk.

Dingieshowe

MAP PAGE 60
A960, KW17 2QQ. Open 24hr. Free.

A small car park (signposted "toilets" in massive capital

Kirkwall and around

Eday, Sanday, Stronsay, Westray

CAFÉ	
The Kirk Café	1

ACCOMMODATION	
Ardconnel B&B	1
Castaway Guesthouse	3
Heatherlea	
Kirkwall Youth Hostel	4
The Lynnfield Hotel	6
Royal Oak Guesthouse	5

Shapinsay
Shapinsay Ferry Terminal
Helliar Holms
Bay of Sandgarth
Newlot
Car Ness
Bay of Carness
Head of Work
Northlink Ferry Terminal
Bay of Kirkwall
Work
Shapinsay Sound
Kirkwall Ferry Terminal
Bay of Meil
Head of Holland
Yinstay Head
Rerwick Head
SEE KIRKWALL MAP FOR DETAILS
Kirkwall
Inganess Bay
Aikers
Boondatoon
Loch of Tankerness
Mull Head
Berstane
The Ness
Mull Head Nature Res.
Highland Park Whisky Distillery
Scapa
Tankerness
Tradespark
Deer Sound
The Gloup
Scapa Bay
Kirkwall Airport
Slap of Toab
Mill Sand
Halley
Skaill
Sandside Bay
DEERNESS
St Clair Farm
Mainland
Braebuster
Gritley
Sebay Farm
Myrtle Cotttage
New Holland
Toab
St Peter's Bay
Stonehall
Newark Bay
North Dawn
Gears
Dingieshowe
Biggings
Springfield
Corn Holm
Bay of Sandoyne
St Mary's
Hurtiso Farm
Warthill 88 m
NORTH SEA
St Mary's Bay
Lamb Holm
Cornquoy
N
0 kilometres 2
0 mile 1
Glims Holm
Northfield
Rose Ness
Warebanks
Aberdeen, Lerwick

SHOP	
The Orkney Furniture Maker	1

A walk at Mull Head

Starting at the car park, a path leads just a few hundred metres to the gloup, a precipitous chasm at the bottom of which you can see a small arch sculpted by the the sea pounding against the cliffs. From here, continue along the grassy track on the cliff edge until you reach the Brough of Deerness, a dramatic crag largely cut off from the Mainland. On the summit are the ruins of an ancient Norse church. At time of writing, the Brough was not accessible due to landslide damage to the path – until this is repaired, you will have to be content with admiring the broch from afar. Note the clear layers of rock in the Brough's cliff – a nod to the headland's geological structure.

The shorter walk doubles back from here, while the longer walk traces the cliff edge on an always obvious grassy path, with ample viewpoints of spectacular scenery and opportunities to spot seabirds and seals.

When you reach a post marked '19', you have the option of adding a 45-minute out-and-back diversion to the Covenanters' Memorial, which is clearly visible along the coast. This pays tribute to a group of seventeenth-century religious dissenters who were sentenced to transportation to the Americas, but were drowned when the ship carrying them hit the rocks on the Deerness peninsula. Once you've seen it, retrace your footsteps to point 19 and take the route heading inland. Turn right at the fence and then left onto the gravel road; follow this back to the car park.

letters, rather than something more enticing such as "beach" or "historical site") off the A960 provides access to **Dingieshowe**, a collection of mounds and sand dunes that Orkney's Norse inhabitants used as a form of parliament. In 1135, it was the venue for a battle between Earl Paul the Silent and his rival Earl Rognvald.

Today, the beach – on the other side of the dunes behind those all-important toilets – is rather more serene; a lovely stretch of white sand and rolling foam-tipped surf.

The next bay to the east, Newark Bay, is also a lovely sandy beach, which looks across to the small island of Copinsay – a designated a Special Protection Area for its breeding seabirds. Uninhabited since 1958, it may be possible to visit by prior arrangement with RSPB Scotland.

Mull Head

MAP PAGE 60
Off B9050, KW17 2QJ.
Open 24hr. Free.

The remote Deerness peninsula ends at **Mull Head**, which makes a good place for a wind-tousled walk (see box, above), taking in fine cliff scenery and a couple of interesting sights, including a dramatic gloup and an ancient church sat atop the precipitous Brough of Deerness. Keen walkers can extend their stroll to reach the Covenanters' Memorial, a tribute to the seventeenth-century religious dissenters who died here.

There's an abundance of seabirds nesting in the cliffs, and seals are often spotted in the water. A visitor centre by the car park offers an overview of the local archeology, natural history and geology, and also displays some lovely photography of the area.

Shops

The Brig Larder

MAP PAGE 58
1 Albert St, KW15 1HP
☎ 01856 873146, ⓦ jollysoforkney.
co.uk/pages/the-brig-larder. Mon–Fri
8.30am–5.30pm, Sat 9am–5pm.
Self-caterers rejoice – this excellent
deli stocks a huge variety of
Orkney produce, from cheese,
meat and fish to pickles and
chutneys. It's also a marvellous
place to pick up local whisky,
gin and rum (tasters available),
and there's a small kitchenware
section if you're looking for a more
permanent souvenir of your trip.

Judith Glue

MAP PAGE 58
25 Broad St, KW15 1DH
☎ 01856 874225, ⓦ judithglue.com.
Mon–Sat 9am–6pm, Sun 11am–4pm.
An extensive souvenir shop
selling Orkney-themed goods of
all descriptions: biscuits, whisky,
pottery, t-shirts, hats, knitwear,
cushions, coasters – you name it,
they've got it. The shop's resident
dog, Selkie, is a delight.

Orcadian Bookshop

MAP PAGE 58
14 Albert St, KW15 1HP
☎ 01856 878000, ⓦ orcadian.co.uk/shop.
Mon–Fri 9am–5pm, Sat 10am–5pm.
If you're looking for a book
covering almost any aspect of life
on Orkney, you're sure to find it
here: the entire right-hand wall
of the shop is packed with local
interest titles. There's also a good
selection of fiction here, ensuring
you'll never be short of reading
matter on your trip.

The Orkney Furniture Maker

MAP PAGE 60
Work Rd, KW15 1UF
☎ 01856 871314, ⓦ orkneyfurniture.co.uk.
Mon–Fri 9am–5pm.
Orkney has a distinctive
traditional chair made of wood
and straw, sometimes including
a hood and integrated drawers,
which you're likely to see in
heritage centres and museums
across the islands. If you're
particularly taken with them,
then fear not, you can acquire
one of your very own from
The Orkney Furniture Maker,

The Brig Larder

Judith Glue

which specializes in producing marvellous traditional chairs, as well as other very high-quality pieces of furniture.

Restaurants

Dil Se

MAP PAGE 58
7 Bridge St, KW15 1HR
☎ 01856 875242, ⓦ dilse-orkney.co.uk.
Daily noon–2pm & 4.30–10.30pm.
Popular and attractively decorated Indian restaurant that specializes in Balti dishes – the chicken *methi* is particularly recommended – but also does all the old favourites as well as several more unusual choices. It's open a little later than many places in Kirkwall, so it's a good choice if you've arrived in town late. ££

Lucano

MAP PAGE 58
31 Victoria St, KW15 1DN
☎ 01856 875687, ⓦ lucanokirkwall.co.uk.
Daily 7.30am–9pm.
Very popular Italian joint with a great selection of pizza and pasta, as well as a regularly changing board of specials focused on local dishes with an Italian twist – Orkney goose breast in porcini mushroom sauce with garlic, pesto and béchamel, for example, or spaghetti with mussels and tomato sauce. The wine list is good, and it's also a decent place to get breakfast. The downside? It's a tad on the pricey side for what it is. £££

Twenty One

MAP PAGE 58
21 Albert Street, KW15 1HQ
ⓦ twentyonetakeaway.co.uk.
Mon & Tues 11am–5pm, Wed 11am–11pm, Thurs 5–11pm, Fri & Sat 11am–1am.
This excellent restaurant on Kirkwall's main drag brings a range of international options to the table, with Mexican quesadillas, Thai *tom pha jai* and Louisiana po' boy (meaty sandwich) all putting in a much-appreciated appearance. It's a good choice at lunchtime, and if you're looking for a lively night out, you'll be pleased to learn *Twenty One* is also home to Kirkwall's most extensive cocktail menu, ensuring it's a popular spot well into the evening. ££

KIRKWALL

Cafés

Archive Coffee

MAP PAGE 58

8 Laing St, KW15 1NW ⓦ facebook.
com/ArchiveCoffeeKirkwall. Mon–Sat
8.30am–5pm, Sun 11am–4pm.

After a very smart, vaguely
industrial makeover, the town's
former library has been reimagined
as one of Kirkwall's most popular
cafés. The menu covers (very
good) open sandwiches, salads and
burgers, plus some options you've
probably never even considered
before: a hot dog topped with
bacon, pulled pork and macaroni
cheese, for example. The titular
coffee is excellent too. ££

The Daily Scoop

MAP PAGE 58

42 Broad St, KW15 1DG ⓣ 01856 877811,
ⓦ facebook.com/thedailyscooporkney.
Daily 10am–5pm.

Occupying a prime spot on the
main square opposite St Magnus
Cathedral, *The Daily Scoop* is an
excellent ice cream parlour with
a huge selection of flavours. If ice
cream's not your thing, crepes are

also available, and the tiffins are
delicious too. Those determined to
avoid sugar overload will enjoy the
home-made cheese scones. £

The Kirk Café

MAP PAGE 60

Off Shore Rd, Tankerness, KW17 2QT
ⓣ 01856 861758, ⓦ sheilafleet.com/
pages/the-kirk-gallery-cafe-orkney.
Mon–Sat 10am–5pm, Sun 11am–5pm.

In a converted church on the
Tankerness peninsula just east of
Kirkwall, this great café is a perfect
spot for lunch (the vegetable daal
is excellent) or just a coffee and
cake (the raspberry meringue
is recommended). Also in the
building is the highly regarded
Sheila Fleet jewellery store, so you
can combine your lunch with a
shopping trip. Afterwards, enjoy a
short walk along the shore of the
nearby Loch of Tankerness. ££

Pubs

Helgi's

MAP PAGE 58

14 Harbour St, KW15 1LE
ⓣ 01856 879293, ⓦ facebook.com/Helgis.

Archive Coffee

Helgi's

Sun & Wed 3–11pm, Thurs 3pm–midnight, Fri & Sat noon–1am.
This deservedly popular seafront pub, named after a leading character in the Orkneyinga Saga, serves up excellent food covering both classic pub grub (fish and chips, macaroni cheese) and more international choices (chicken fajitas, butternut squash risotto). It has a strong burger menu, with the "Old Man of Hoy" (piled high with bacon, cheese, and black pudding) taking some beating. There's a tempting selection of Orcadian beers, whiskies and gins too. All in all, it's one of the best places in town for grub, so booking ahead is strongly advised. ££

Royal Cask Whisky Gin Bar

MAP PAGE 58
40 Victoria St, KW15 1DN
ⓘ 01856 873477,
Ⓦ orkneyhotel.co.uk/drink. **Sun–Thurs 5–11pm, Fri & Sat 5pm–midnight.**
The bar of the *Orkney Hotel* may call itself a "whisky gin bar", but the gin doesn't get much of a look-in after you catch sight of the bewildering menu of whiskies that runs to more than five pages. Staff are extremely knowledgeable on the various distilleries, so it's a good place to work out which whisky suits you best. It's a fun bar when it's lively, but on quieter evenings it can lack atmosphere. ££

St Ola Hotel

MAP PAGE 58
Harbour St, KW15 1LE
ⓘ 01856 875090, Ⓦ stolahotel.co.uk.
Mon–Thurs 11am–midnight, Fri 11am–1am, Sat 10am–1am, Sun 10am–midnight.
This place – easily spotted on the waterfront and within a short stumbling distance of the Northern Isles ferry port – is a veritable Kirkwall institution. An inn of some sort is thought to have occupied this spot for perhaps 500 years, though after numerous renovations and modernizations, it's hard to tell that it's particularly historic. Service is occasionally a bit patchy, but the food is good, with plenty of classic pub grub and a fine range of hearty burgers, as well as an excellent dessert menu. ££

Burray and South Ronaldsay

Once separate islands but now connected to each other and Orkney's Mainland by the Churchill Barriers, Burray and South Ronaldsay stretch out southwards towards John O'Groats. There are a couple of interesting prehistoric sites and some lovely coastal walking here, but the jewel in these islands' crown is its wartime heritage. As well as the Churchill Barriers themselves, the most impressive relic of World War II is the Italian Chapel, a beautiful church built and decorated by bored but talented Italian prisoners of war.

Burray

You'll need to drive over three Churchill Barriers (see box, page 67) to reach Burray from the Mainland, as there are two small islands in between: Lamb Holm and Glimps Holm. Lamb Holm is where you'll find one of Orkney's highlights, the remarkable Italian Chapel. On Burray itself, there's an excellent museum, a beautiful beach, and – rather unexpectedly – a Viking totem pole.

Italian Chapel

MAP PAGE 68
A961, Lamb Holm, KW17 2SF
Ⓦ facebook.com/italianchapelorkney.
9am–6.30pm. Charge.

Unquestionably one of Orkney's top sights, the **Italian Chapel** was built during World War II by Italian prisoners of war who were here to work on the construction of the Churchill Barriers. It's found on the site of Camp 60, where many Italians, including Moena-born painter Domenico Chiocchetti,

The Italian Chapel was built by Italian POWs in World War II

Churchill Barriers

Six weeks after the outbreak of World War II, a German U-boat managed to evade Scapa Flow's defences to enter the harbour, attacking HMS *Royal Oak*. The ship sank, and 834 lives were lost. As Scapa Flow was Britain's most important harbour, the evident lack of security was deeply concerning, and in response Winston Churchill ordered that Scapa Flow be defended from enemy attack by constructing enormous barriers between the islands on the east side of the harbour. The project presented huge engineering challenges, involving the placement of nearly a million tons of rock and concrete, which took from May 1940 until September 1944 to complete. Much of the work was undertaken by Italian prisoners of war, who initially went on strike on the basis that the Geneva Convention prohibited prisoners from undertaking work to aid the opposing side's war effort. This was resolved when it was determined that the barriers were in fact civilian causeways to link the islands. This is certainly how the barriers are now used today: roads cross each barrier, allowing access from the Orkney Mainland to Lamb Holm, Glimps Holm, Burray and South Ronaldsay.

were interned. Chiocchetti's artistic skills initially found an outlet with the creation of a statue of St George and the Dragon, which can still be seen on site, but the circumstance of the camp inhabitants' need for a chapel meant that he could go on to create his masterpiece, aided by many other prisoners with considerable talent.

The shell of the chapel is made from two huts joined together, with their corrugated iron walls plastered over and exquisitely painted to resemble brickwork and a vaulted ceiling. Around the doorway, there's a depiction of elaborate pillars, panels and a quatrefoil with the letters HIS, a representation of the name Jesus in Greek.

The painting at the altar is heavy with symbolism, all of it depicting the need for peace: the Baby Jesus holds an olive branch, surrounded by angels bearing the words "Regina Pacis, ora pro nobis", meaning "Queen of Peace, pray for us". Another angel sheathes a sword, while a fourth bears the shield of Moena, Chiocchetti's hometown.

The chapel was not completed before the war ended, but Chiocchetti remained behind to finish his work. He and many other former prisoners retained their links with Orkney and the chapel for the rest of their lives, returning several times to aid in restoration and to make additions, including the wooden panels around the sides which tell the story of Christ's Passion, gifted to the chapel by Chiocchetti and his wife Maria in 1964.

Fossil and Heritage Centre

MAP PAGE 68
A961, Burray, KW17 2SY
ⓦ orkneyfossilcentre.co.uk.
May–Sept Tues–Sun 10am–5pm. Charge.

Burray's **Fossil and Heritage Centre** is a well-presented and extensive museum, with a fantastic range of fossils found both in Orkney and around the world. The first room has a particularly fine collection of fishy fossils, as well as engaging explanations of geological history that explain how fossils are formed, while the second

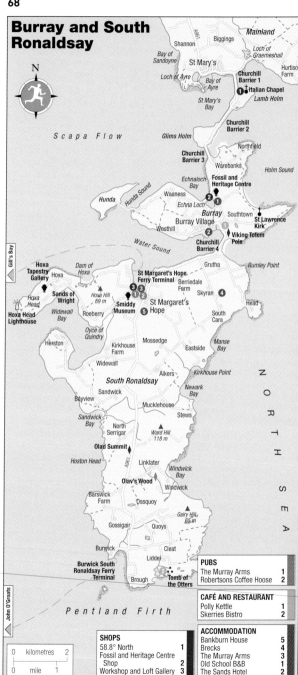

room has a marvellous display of ammonites, crystals and a few dinosaur fossils.

If you prefer your history a little more modern, there's a wealth of information here on the attack on HMS *Royal Oak* and the subsequent construction of the Churchill Barriers, and the large floor map helps demonstrate Scapa Flow's geography. The museum also holds ethnographic displays featuring everyday items from Orkney's past – look out in particular for the diary of Bessie Bechan, who recorded her views of the happenings in Orkney throughout World War II.

On site too is an archive room, including old resources such as census records, maps, wartime documents, and a small library of local interest books. It may be of particular use if you're researching your family history.

St Lawrence Kirk

MAP PAGE 68
Ness Rd, Burray, KW17 2TA.
Open 24hr. Free.
The infrequently visited ruins of **St Lawrence Kirk** are surrounded by a well-maintained cemetery that contains some Commonwealth war graves. The church itself is thought to date back at least to the twelfth century, and intriguingly was in the early 1700s home to a canoe of Inuit origin. It's a lovely peaceful spot, offering fine views along the sandy beach of Bu and across to Cornquoy.

Viking Totem Pole

MAP PAGE 68
Off A961, Burray, KW17 2TA.
Open 24hr. Free.
At the north end of the fourth Churchill Barrier, a small car park offers access through the dunes to a pleasant beach of white sand and turquoise waters – if you catch it on a sunny day. Near the car park is a slightly curious **totem pole** with a Viking head at the top.

St Margarets Hope

South Ronaldsay

The largest settlement on **South Ronaldsay** is the charming village of St Margaret's Hope, on the island's northern coast, which makes a relaxed base if you want to spend a couple of days in this corner of Orkney. The island is home to some beautiful coastline and beaches, some interesting wartime remains on Hoxa Head, and a pair of prehistoric tombs.

Smiddy Museum

MAP PAGE 68
School Rd, St Margaret's Hope, South Ronaldsay, KW17 2TP
Ⓦ **facebook.com/smiddymuseum.**
April–Sept Mon–Sat 2–4.30pm. Charge.
In the village's old smithy, and labelled outside as W. Hourston Blacksmith Museum, the **Smiddy** is packed full of blacksmithing tools, many of which are the originals that were left here when the smithy closed in the 1960s. The immense bellows in the back room are particularly impressive. The museum also holds a small exhibition on local history, primarily concerned with the tradition of the Horse Ploughing

Match, in which children dress in colourful costumes based on horse harnesses and compete to be the best at ploughing an area of the local beach. The event is still held annually on the third Saturday in August, so if your visit coincides, be sure to attend.

Sands of Wright

MAP PAGE 68
B9043, South Ronaldsay, KW17 2TW.
Open 24hr. Free.

The small but pretty **Sands of Wright** are the venue for St Margaret Hope's annual ploughing competition. From here, you can follow a short path through a patch of woodland and past a small loch to the Howe of Hoxa, a semi-excavated cairn. Unconfirmed report has it that this is the burial place of the tenth-century Earl of Orkney Thorfinn Skullsplitter, who was clearly a lovely chap if nominative determinism is anything to go by. You can extend your walk on a circular route to the other side of the headland and then back to the Sands of Wright.

Hoxa Tapestry Art Gallery

MAP PAGE 68
Off B9043, South Ronaldsay, KW17 2TW
Ⓦ hoxatapestrygallery.co.uk. April–Sept
Mon–Fri 10am–5.30pm, Sun 2–5pm. Free.

One of Orkney's most interesting art destinations, the **Hoxa Tapestry Art Gallery** displays the work of mother and daughter Leila and Jo Thomson, who produce tapestries and art prints inspired by the landscapes of Orkney. When visiting, you can often see works in progress, as well as the finished articles.

Hoxa Head

MAP PAGE 68
Off B9043, South Ronaldsay, KW17 2TW.
Open 24hr. Free.

As the main entrance to Scapa Flow, the waters off South Ronaldsay's northwest tip long had major strategic importance, a fact that's evident from the ruins of the gun batteries from both World Wars that can be found on **Hoxa Head**. A short circular walk from a handy car park takes you up to and through the wartime remains, while also providing gorgeous views across Orkney's southern islands and across to the Scottish mainland. This is also a good walk for nature lovers: there's a profusion of bird life here, and sightings of porpoises, orcas and minke whales are not uncommon.

Olav's Wood

MAP PAGE 68
Off A961, South Ronaldsay, KW17 2RN
Ⓦ olavswood.org.uk. Open 24hr. Free.

Trees are in general conspicuous by their absence on Orkney, so it's something of a pleasure to go for a short walk in this small planned woodland. Multiple trails, named

The scuttling of the German Fleet

In the aftermath of World War I, seventy-four ships from the German fleet were brought to Scapa Flow, where they were to stay until peace negotiations were concluded on 21 June 1919. The fleet's commander, Vice-Admiral Ludwig von Reuter, believed war would resume and was determined to ensure that the ships would not be acquired by the Allies without the permission of the German government. Unaware that an extension to the conference until 23 June had been agreed, von Reuter gave the order to scuttle the fleet on the morning of 21 June. Fifty of the seventy-four ships sank, and the remainder were beached. Over the course of the twentieth century, most of the ships were salvaged, but seven remain in Scapa Flow and are now often explored by divers.

Hoxa Head

after the people who planted them, run around sections of differing tree species. The deeper you delve into the woods, the darker the paths become – by the time you're in the conifer maze, it's almost sinister. **Olav's Wood** is perhaps not an essential stop, but worth it if you have time.

A short distance north, on the A961, is **Olad Summit**, a high spot from which you can enjoy a panoramic view taking in the Scottish mainland across to Hoy and Flotta, and round to the west end of the Orkney Mainland.

Tomb of the Otters

MAP PAGE 68
Cleat, South Ronaldsay, KW17 2RW
☏ 01856 831605,
🌐 tomboftheotters.co.uk. Tues–Thurs 11am–4pm, by guided tour only. Charge.
A relatively recent archeological find, the **Tomb of the Otters** is a neolithic tomb discovered in 2010. Dug out of solid rock, it has not yet been fully excavated, but the chambers that have been explored contain not only human remains, but otter bones as well – hence the name. The presence of the otters

suggests that the tomb was not tightly sealed while it was in use, allowing the creatures to come and go as they pleased.

Nearby is the Tomb of the Eagles, a similarly impressive site, but unfortunately this is now closed to the public, with no plans for reopening at time of writing.

Burwick

MAP PAGE 68
The foot passenger from John O'Groats arrives at **Burwick**, a small hamlet at the southern tip of South Ronaldsay. It's of limited interest, though the local church contains a stone featuring a pair of footprints: locals will tell you a story about these which involves St Magnus and a sea monster, but less excitingly the reality is more likely to be that this was a Pictish coronation stone.

The five-mile footpath that traces the western side of South Ronaldsay starts/ends here, though as there's no public transport (a fact of which the information board sounds inordinately proud), you'll need to arrange for somebody to pick you up if you don't want to walk there and back.

Shops

58.8° North

MAP PAGE 68
A961, Lamb Holm, KW17 2SF
☎ 01856 781736, Ⓦ jgowrum.com.
Mon–Sat 10am–3pm (Fri till 2pm).

If you're looking for a souvenir that's a little out the ordinary, you could do worse than picking up a bottle of rum made here on Orkney. Named after the infamous pirate John Gow, there are three different award-winning rums available here. If rum's not your thing, local liqueur, wines and whisky are also on sale, as well as non-alcoholic products such as shortbread and chocolate.

Fossil and Heritage Centre Shop

MAP PAGE 68
A961, Burray, KW17 2SY ☎ 01856 731255,
Ⓦ orkneyfossilcentre.co.uk.
May–Sept Tues–Sun 10am–5pm.

The shop attached to the Fossil and Heritage Centre offers a fine selection of souvenirs such as pottery, glassware and jewellery. You'll also find tea towels, coasters and fridge magnets, as well as a decent range of local interest books, and a good selection of fossil-themed toys.

Workshop and Loft Gallery

MAP PAGE 68
Front Rd, St Margaret's Hope, South Ronaldsay, KW17 2SL ☎ 01856 831587,
Ⓦ workshopandloftgallery.co.uk.
Tues–Sat 10am–5pm.

A fantastic little shop selling a fine range of locally produced items, the most prominent of which is the handknitted clothing. Other excellent products include some stunning glassware, and there's a fine selection of artworks too, from watercolours to etchings. It's easy to find a great souvenir here.

Restaurant

Skerries Bistro

MAP PAGE 68
Cleat, South Ronaldsay, KW17 2RW
☎ 01856 831605, Ⓦ skerriesbistro.co.uk.
Mon–Fri 11am–4pm.

An upmarket place at the southern end of South Ronaldsay, *Skerries* specializes in fish and seafood, all caught locally and prepared on site. The lobster is particularly

Fossil and Heritage Centre, Burray

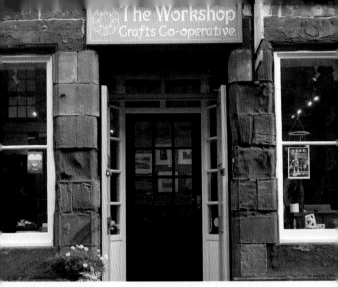

The Workshop and Loft Gallery

good choice, but the scallops with asparagus and the fish chowder are also extremely popular. ££££

Café

Polly Kettle

MAP PAGE 68

A961, Burray, KW17 2SS ☎ 07901 505694, Ⓦ pollykettle.com. Tues–Sun 11am–5pm.
There's a welcome Middle Eastern flavour to the menu at the *Polly Kettle* café, with falafel, tahini, *fuul* and Egyptian milk pudding all putting in an appearance alongside toasties, scones and waffles. The coffee is great, and there's a fine selection of ice-cream flavours. The café doubles as a handicraft shop, offering knitwear, artwork and glassware, all of which make excellent gifts. ££

Pubs

Murray Arms

MAP PAGE 68

Back Rd, St Margaret's Hope, South Ronaldsay, KW17 2SP ☎ 01856 831205, Ⓦ themurrayarmshotel.com. April–Sept

Sun–Thurs noon–11pm, Fri & Sat noon–midnight; Oct–March Mon & Thurs 4–10pm, Fri & Sat noon–midnight, Sun noon–10pm.
If fish and seafood are your thing, this is the place to go: the menu is locally sourced ocean products from beginning to end. From crab to mussels by way of salmon and scallops, there's plenty to pick from – and if you can't choose, there's a seafood platter that offers something of everything. £££

Robertsons Coffee Hoose

MAP PAGE 68

Church Rd, St Margaret's Hope, South Ronaldsay, KW17 2SR ☎ 01856 831889, Ⓦ robertsonscoffeehooseandbar.com. Fri & Sat noon–1am, Sun & Thurs noon–10pm.
More than just a coffeehouse, *Robertsons* is a strong contender for best bar on Orkney. It's somehow got the air of an old-fashioned apothecary, with bottles and tea sets stacked on the high shelves behind the beautiful wooden bar, and the impression is completed by the black-and-white tiled floor. It's a friendly place for a drink and serves top-notch food – what more could you want? Highly recommended. ££

Rousay, Egilsay and Wyre

The sea channel known as Eynhallow Sound separates Orkney's west Mainland from Rousay, Egilsay and Wyre, a trio of islands notable for its enormous historical significance. Rousay, the largest of the three, rewards in-depth exploration of its huge number of neolithic sites, including the beautiful Midhowe Broch and the vast adjacent Midhowe Cairn. Egilsay, meanwhile, is home to perhaps Orkney's single most important medieval site, St Magnus Church, built on the spot where Magnus was martyred in 1117, while the diminutive Wyre is worth a visit for the small but fascinating ruins of Cubbie Roo's Castle.

Rousay

The largest of the islands on the Eynhallow Sound, Rousay makes an excellent day-trip from Mainland. It possesses a disproportionate number of interesting archeological sites, and a couple of good walking routes. Physically, the island feels different too: more rugged and uncompromising than the soft rolling hills on Mainland. Essentially one big hill encircled by a ring road, it's easy to get around by car, bike or on foot. The sites below are described in a clockwise direction from the ferry terminal.

Rousay Heritage Centre

MAP PAGE 76
Rousay Pier, Rousay, KW17 2PU.
Daily 9am–6pm. Free.

The modest **Rousay Heritage Centre**, which moonlights as the ferry waiting room, has a very small collection of replicas of local archeological finds, but what it lacks in exhibits it makes up for in engaging information boards, covering many of Rousay's sights in depth.

You'll also find a helpful leaflet here that describes a number of short walks on Rousay, Egilsay and Wyre.

Taversöe Tuick

MAP PAGE 76
B9064, Rousay, KW17 2PR
Ⓦ historicenvironment.scot/visit-a-place/places/taversoee-tuick-chambered-cairn.
Open 24hr. Free.

A rarity among Orkney cairns, **Taversöe Tuick** is two storeys high. Entering through a passage onto the upper floor (now roofed by a concrete dome), you can then descend to the lower level via an

Reaching Rousay

Most of Orkney's island ferries leave from Kirkwall, but services to Rousay, Egilsay and Wyre are among the exceptions: to get here, you'll need to head north from Finstown to the tiny settlement of Tingwall. Up to six daily ferries leave Tingwall for Rousay, a journey that usually takes 25 minutes. If you're driving, note that you'll have to reverse on to the ferry. Services from Tingwall to Rousay will usually then continue on to Egilsay or Wyre, making it possible to visit two out of the three in one day.

The Clearances

Orkney was for the most part spared the effects of the Highland Clearances, the large-scale eviction of crofters and tenants on estates owned by powerful landlords, but many of those living on Rousay in the late 1800s were affected. At the time, Frederick Traill-Burroughs was the landowner, and in order to finance the construction of Trumland House, he increased rents, evicting any tenant that could not pay. Despite complaints made against him, and a Royal Commission investigation, Traill-Burroughs was adamant in his policy. The island's population fell dramatically, and is today less than a fifth of its nineteenth-century peak.

iron ladder. The skylight in the dome ensures it remains light inside, so it's easier to see what's what in here than in many of Orkney's cairns.

Looking east from the cairn, you'll see the grey and austere lines of Trumland House. Once home to Frederick Traill-Burroughs (see box, above), the gardens were once open to the public, but at the time of writing were not accepting visitors.

Blackhammer Chambered Cairn

MAP PAGE 76
B9064, Rousay, KW17 2PT

Taversöe Tuick

Ⓦ historicenvironment.scot/visit-a-place/ places/blackhammer-chambered-cairn. Open 24hr. Free.

A long and thin burial mound, **Blackhammer Chambered Cairn** is accessed via a sliding hatch on the roadward side. Inside, the cairn's huddle of seven compartments is still clear, but a strange impression is given by the protective concrete dome with circular skylight windows, which was installed in the 1930s: it makes the tomb feel somehow space age, as if it were the result of neolithic people building a nuclear bunker.

Knowe of Yarso Chambered Cairn

MAP PAGE 76
B9064, Rousay, KW17 2PT
Ⓦ historicenvironment.scot/visit-a-place/
places/knowe-of-yarso-chambered-cairn.
Open 24hr. Free.

As the tourist literature puts it, this is a tomb with a view – at sixty metres above sea level, it's Orkney's highest. From the signposted car park, take the farm track uphill and branch left at the sign, then follow the obvious path to the cairn, which is just below the top of the ridge. From here, there's a fantastic view of the Eynhallow Sound and West Mainland. Inside, the stones are green with algae, and stalactites are emerging from the ceiling of the 1930s concrete dome. All in all, the **Knowe of Yarso Chambered Cairn** is an atmospheric place that's well worth the climb to reach.

Midhowe Chambered Cairn

MAP PAGE 76
B9064, Rousay, KW17 2PS
Ⓦ historicenvironment.scot/visit-a-place/
places/midhowe-chambered-cairn.
Open 24hr. Free.

Excavated in the 1930s by Walter Grant of the Highland Park Whisky Distillery, the **Midhowe Chambered Cairn** is an enormous burial mound concealing twelve chambers. Built 5400 years ago, the tomb holds the remains of twenty-five people, as well as those of animals. The cairn is now housed in a hangar building, and you can walk on gangways above the tomb.

Midhowe Broch

MAP PAGE 76
B9064, Rousay, KW17 2PS
Ⓦ historicenvironment.scot/visit-a-place/
places/midhowe-broch. Open 24hr. Free.

Just next door to the Midhowe Chambered Cairn is **Midhowe**

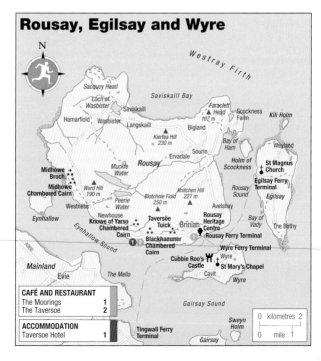

Rousay, Egilsay and Wyre

CAFÉ AND RESTAURANT	
The Moorings	1
The Taversoe	2

ACCOMMODATION	
Taversoe Hotel	1

Rousay's heritage trail

From the Midhowe Chambered Cairn (see opposite), it's possible to follow a path east along the coast that takes in a string of historical sites in rapid succession. Within a few hundred metres of Midhowe, you'll come to Brough Farm, established in the Viking period. A short distance again are the tumbledown ruins of the Wirk, which was quite possibly the Hall of Sigurd in the Orkneyinga Saga, where Earl Paul the Silent was kidnapped by his enemy, Svein Asleifsson, and subsequently murdered.

Just next door to the Wirk are the lichen-covered ruins of St Mary's Church, which dates from the Viking period, though the present building is probably sixteenth century. Next up are the remnants of the buildings of Skaill Farm, which contains the remains of a stone kiln.

Unless you're especially dedicated, it is best to retrace your footsteps from Skaill Farm, as the trail from here becomes extremely indistinct. If you do wish to continue, there are several red-herring paths: you need the one that leads down towards the coast from Skaill Farm's last building and passes round a V-shaped fence at the end of the wall. You'll find yourself on shingle: climb up this to the ridge and follow the path, which comes and goes, to the Knowe of Swandro, a neolithic tomb that's under threat from the sea. Nearby are the scant remains of a Norse Hall.

The trail is allegedly circular, but from the Norse Hall it's very challenging to work out which way to go: paths appear and disappear, and you can find yourself repeatedly coming up against walls, fences and marshy ground. Your aim should be to reach Longness Farm and head up the trail to the road from there, but the best option is probably to return the way you came.

With all these historic sites, including the Midhowe Chambered Cairn and Broch, strung along this shoreline, it's small wonder that this area is considered one of the most archeologically rich miles in Scotland. Even without the historical interest, though, it's a lovely walk with sublime coastal views and a good chance of wildlife sightings: there's a fine array of birdlife, and seals are common here in the early summer.

Broch, an Iron Age tower that was constructed in the first century AD. It's remarkable to think that, even though the broch is two thousand years old, the neighbouring cairn was already 3500 years old at the time the broch was built.

Situated in a magnificently elemental spot on the shoreline overlooking the Eynhallow Sound, the broch is protected by 3m-high walls. Inside, the hearth and a grindstone are clearly visible, as are internal walls, substantial alcoves, and dark rooms in the exterior wall. It's thought that the owners of this broch were well-off: excavators here found bronze ornaments and Samian pottery from the Roman Empire.

Outside the tower are the remains of smaller buildings, all surrounded by a defensive ditch. Nowadays, the broch is defended by the 1930s sea wall, which was erected to save the structure from damage caused by coastal erosion.

Midhowe Broch

Sacquoy Head

MAP PAGE 76
Off B9064, Rousay, KW17 2PS.
Open 24hr. Free.

For great views of Orkney's Mainland, you can take an out-and-back walk to **Sacquoy Head**, in Rousay's northwest corner. The path starts from Sacquoy Farm, at the northwest edge of the Loch of Wasbister. There's no parking, so you may wish to extend the walk by starting from Nousty Sand at the loch's northeast corner, where there's a small parking area at the beach. Seals are often spotted here.

Faraclett Head

MAP PAGE 76
Off B9064, Rousay, KW17 2PR.
Open 24hr. Free.

Rousay's northeast corner offers an enjoyable two-mile circular walk across fields and around the coastline, from which there are good views of Rousay and across to Egilsay. Start at the car park at **Faraclett Head**. On this walk, you'll also catch a glimpse of Yetnasteen, a standing stone that legend claims is a petrified giant that comes to life every New Year's Eve for long enough to head over to the Loch of Scockness for a drink.

Egilsay

Egilsay, cast adrift on the east side of Rousay, is a small island that boasts huge historical significance: it was here that St Magnus (see page 57) was martyred in the early twelfth century. The church dedicated to him is the island's main sight; with a bit of planning, it's possible to take this in on the same day as a visit to Rousay.

Reaching Egilsay and Wyre

Ferries between Rousay and Egilsay (5 daily) usually originate in Tingwall, so you can sail from Tingwall to Rousay, explore the island, then continue to Egilsay, or go straight from Tingwall to Egilsay via Rousay. Services between Rousay and Wyre (4 daily) also originate in Tingwall, affording you the same flexibility.

St Magnus Way

The St Magnus Way is a 58-mile marked route taking in a string of historical sites related to Orkney's favourite martyr (see page 57). The trail starts on Egilsay, but thereafter is confined to Mainland, running from Evie to Kirkwall via Birsay, Dounby and Orphir. Sites along the way include Egilsay's St Magnus Church, the Broch of Gurness and, of course, Kirkwall's St Magnus Cathedral. Detailed information on the route is available at ⓦ stmagnusway.com.

St Magnus Church

MAP PAGE 76
Egilsay, KW17 2QD ⓦ historicenvironment.scot/visit-a-place/places/st-magnus-church-egilsay. Open 24hr. Free.

Magnus, Earl of Orkney, was murdered on Egilsay in around 1117, and approximately twenty years later, he was canonized by Bishop William (see page 57). It's thought to have been around this time that the distinctive stone **St Magnus Church** was built on Egilsay, apparently on the site of his martyrdom. Now in ruins, the church retains its impressive round tower, and enjoys an enviable position with views across to Rousay.

Wyre

The smallest of the Eynhallow Sound ensemble, **Wyre** has a couple of interesting historic sites that reward a quick visit – taking the afternoon ferry from Rousay to Wyre and then the early evening ferry from Wyre to Tingwall should give you all the time you need.

St Mary's Chapel

MAP PAGE 76
Wyre, KW17 2QA ⓦ historicenvironment.scot/visit-a-place/places/cubbie-roos-castle-and-st-marys-chapel.
Open 24hr. Free.

In the centre of Wyre are the ruins of **St Mary's Chapel**, a small church thought to have been founded by Bjarni Kolbeinsson, the Bishop of Orkney, in the twelfth century. In 1933, an impressive piece of medieval iron armour was discovered here. The neighbouring farmhouse, the Bu, is the childhood home of the poet Edwin Muir.

Cubbie Roo's Castle

MAP PAGE 76
Wyre, KW17 2QA ⓦ historicenvironment.scot/visit-a-place/places/cubbie-roos-castle-and-st-marys-chapel.
Open 24hr. Free.

Just south of St Mary's, you'll find the **castle** of a Viking chieftain called Kolbeinn Hrúga, later corrupted to the rather sweet-sounding Cubbie Roo. Though now largely in ruins, the original design is still possible to make out. According to the Orkneyinga Saga, Cubbie Roo built this castle to live in, but it is more likely he used it solely for the defence of the Eynhallow Sound while living more comfortably elsewhere in the vicinity.

St Magnus Church

Only a few hostels and campsites are to be found on Rousay

Restaurant

Taversoe Hotel
MAP PAGE 76
B9064, Rousay, KW17 2PT
☏ 01856 821325,
🌐 taversoehotel.co.uk. Tues–Sun 5–9pm.
With great views across the Eynhallow Sound to the Mainland, the *Taversoe Hotel* is a lovely spot to enjoy dinner. The menu is small but good, with fish and chips the top choice. Food intolerances can be catered for, and there's a surprisingly extensive range of vegetarian options. If you happen to be staying overnight, there's a well-stocked bar here too, offering up a selection of Orcadian beers and whiskies. It's best to book a table in advance, as the restaurant does not always keep its set hours, particularly outside the main tourist season. ££

Café

The Moorings
MAP PAGE 76
Johnstons Rd, Rousay, KW17 2PU
☏ 07956 395725
Mon 11am–2pm, Tues & Wed 11am–2pm & 4–6pm, Thurs–Sat 11am–6pm.
This takeaway van, just behind Rousay Heritage Centre, was at time of writing the only place to get hot food or drinks during the daytime on the island. A smattering of wooden tables outside caters for those who want to sit while they eat. Expect quick and easy eats along the likes of fried egg or bacon rolls, paninis and burgers; later in the day, pizzas are thrown into the mix. It's not always open, even during set hours, so don't rely on it – bringing a picnic to Rousay could be a good option. £

Eating on Egilsay and Wyre

There are no eating establishments on Egilsay or Wyre: if you're planning on spending any length of time on either island, it would be wise to bring a picnic with you.

Westray and Papa Westray

The northern island of Westray is one of Orkney's most popular destinations, with visitors keen to explore its elemental coastal walks – particularly around Noup Head and Castle o'Burrian – as well as historical sites such as Noltland Castle. The main settlement, Pierowall, is a sizeable village that makes an excellent base for exploring the island. From here, you can also hop on the foot passenger ferry across the water to neighbouring Papa Westray, a dinky island that's home to one of Orkney's archeological big-hitters.

Westray

Ask any Orcadian which their favourite of the islands is, and there's a good chance they'll tell you it's **Westray**. It's not hard to see why: Westray is a fantastic destination, boasting gorgeous scenery with particularly fine beaches, marvellous wildlife-spotting opportunities, fascinating history, and a thriving community spirit. Spending several days here is a must for any visit to Orkney.

Southern beaches
MAP PAGE 82

If arriving by ferry, you'll make landfall at the small settlement of Rapness: head south from here on the road signposted to Ness to find a couple of tiny but gorgeous white-sand **beaches**, one just opposite the *Richan's Retreat* café, and another a little further along, beneath an electricity substation. Strewn with jagged black rocks and laced by fine white sand, these are beautiful and seldom-visited spots.

Castle o'Burrian
MAP PAGE 82

From a car park beside a ruined mill – check out its rusting old waterwheel – a path curves around the coast to **Castle o'Burrian**, a blocky and wide sea stack that shelters nesting seabirds, and is thought to once have been home to early Christians too. The route is punctuated by occasional stone waymarkers, but you can't really go too far wrong here: don't stray into the fields to your right, and don't walk off the cliff to your left. Look out for impressive geology as you walk – at some points, you can see dramatic folds in the rock, giving an idea of the enormous forces at work here. Particularly good folds can be seen from near the picnic bench on the promontory behind the mill.

You'll reach Castle o'Burrian after about ten minutes' walk. If you're here in summer, keep an eye out for puffins, which often nest here: the evening is the best time to spot them. If you're enjoying the walk, consider continuing along

Reaching Westray

Daily ferries run from Kirkwall to Westray and back again, taking about an hour and a half. Flights from Kirkwall are roughly twice a week, and take about 25 minutes.

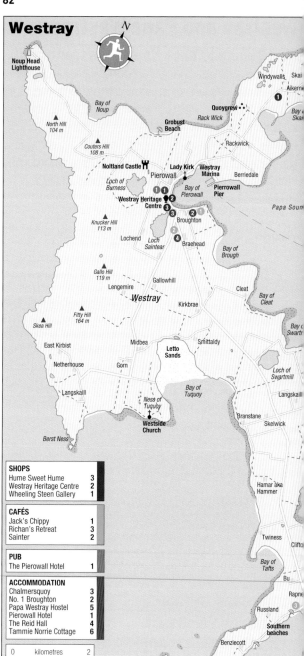

Westray

N

Noup Head Lighthouse

Bay of Noup

North Hill 104 m

Couters Hill 108 m

Windywalls · Skai

Aikern

1

Bay of Skai

Quoygrew · ·

Rack Wick

Grobust Beach

Rackwick

Noltland Castle

Lady Kirk **Westray Marina**

Pierowall

Berriedale

1 **1**

Loch of Burness

Bay of Pierowall

Pierowall Pier

Westray Heritage Centre

3

2 **1**

Papa Soun

3

Broughton

Knucker Hill 113 m

Lochend

Loch Saintear

2

4 **Braehead**

Bay of Brough

Gallo Hill 119 m

Gallowhill

Lengemire

Westray

Kirkbrae

Cleat

Bay of Cleat

Bay o Swartr

Fitty Hill 164 m

Skea Hill

Midbea

Smittaldy

Letto Sands

Bay o Swartm

East Kirbist

Netherhouse

Gorn

Loch of Swartmill

Langskaill

Langskaill

Berst Ness

Ness of Tuquoy

Westside Church

Bay of Tuquoy

Branstane

Skelwick

Hamar aka Hammer

Twiness

Clifto

Bay of Tafts

Bu

Rapne

Russland

3

Southern beaches

Benziecott

Wart Holm

Point of Huro

Kirkwall ▽

SHOPS	
Hume Sweet Hume	3
Westray Heritage Centre	2
Wheeling Steen Gallery	1

CAFÉS	
Jack's Chippy	1
Richan's Retreat	3
Sainter	2

PUB	
The Pierowall Hotel	1

ACCOMMODATION	
Chalmersquoy	3
No. 1 Broughton	2
Papa Westray Hostel	5
Pierowall Hotel	1
The Reid Hall	4
Tammie Norrie Cottage	6

0	kilometres	2

0	mile	1

SEE PAPA WESTRAY
MAP BELOW FOR DETAILS

NORTH HILL

Westray
Airport

Holm
of Aikerness

Papa Westray

Papa Westray
Airport

Holland

Backiskaill

Loch of
St Tredwell

Holm of Papa

Bay of
Moclett

Papa Westray
Ferry Terminal

Spo Ness

Bay of
Hawey

Castle
o'Burrian

angar

Grimbust

estray
rry Terminal

Weather
Ness

Weatherness
Sound

Holm of Faray

Papa Westray

N

NORTH HILL

North Hill RSPB
reserve

Bewan

Whitelooms

Rose Cottage

North Wick

Papa Westray

St Boniface
Kirk

Quoys

Papa Westray
Airport

Skennist

Knap of Howar

The Kelp Store
Heritage and
Art Centre

Bayview

South Wick

Holland

5

John o'Holland's
Bothy Museum

Links

Holm of Papa

Backiskaill

Chapel of
St Tredwell

Loch of
St Tredwell

Peatwell

Bay of
Burland

Bight of
Quoyolie

Windywalls

Charleston

Vestness

Bay of
Moclett

Sheepheight

Papa Westray
Ferry Terminal

| 0 | metres | 1000 |
| 0 | yards | 1000 |

Pierowall

Kirkwall

Whale skeleton in Pierowall

the coast path to enjoy even more picturesque scenery. Take care along the entire walk, though, as there are steep drops and the path does run close to the cliff edge at times.

A little south of Castle o'Burrian, a turning off the main road signposted to Rapness Cemetery leads down a rough but driveable track to a small car park. From here, take a short path down to a wide expanse of gorgeous beach, a long sweep of white sand with clear – and cold – water. On a sunny day, you can believe you're in the Caribbean.

Bay of Swartmill

MAP PAGE 82

Another of Westray's fine beaches, the **Bay of Swartmill** is threaded by white sand and clear water, and is a decent place to spot oystercatchers wading in the shallows. There are good views across to Papa Westray from here.

Letto Sands

MAP PAGE 82

It's perhaps not the prettiest beach you'll ever see, but if you have time to kill, it's worth a stop at **Letto Sands**, which wrap around a wide bay on the island's southwest coast. On a sunny day, the water sparkles in the light, and oystercatchers strut about picking at the sand.

Westside Church

MAP PAGE 82

Westray, KW17 2DR ⓦ historicenvironment. scot/visit-a-place/places/westside-church-tuquoy. Open 24hr. Free.

Also referred to as Tuquoy Church or Cross Kirk, the **Westside Church** is set in an attractive location at the tip of a small peninsula. Likely the work of the twelfth-century nobleman Haflidi Thorkelsson, the Romanesque edifice is one of Orkney's most important medieval church ruins. At time of research, the remains were largely cordoned off awaiting safety inspections and possible renovation.

The church is reached from a car park at the Point o' the Scurroes, from which you'll need to follow an 800m-long path along the coast – wear long trousers, as the trail isn't hugely well maintained and there are nettles aplenty. The path does technically continue from the church, but you'd need a machete to make much headway. If the route gets cleared, it should be possible to follow it from here along the coast to pretty Mae Sands.

Westray Heritage Centre

MAP PAGE 82
Pierowall, Westray, KW17 2BZ
ⓦ westrayheritage.co.uk.
Mon 11.30am–5pm, Tues–Sat 9am–noon, 2–5pm, Sun 1.30–5pm. Charge.

There's a fine display of artefacts from Westray's past at the **Heritage Centre**, found in the centre of Pierowall. Starting with fossils and moving through to the modern day, via neolithic remains, Westray's importance during the Norse era, and the history of kelp farming, the well-presented collection is well worth a browse.

There are numerous highlights to see here, including the Westray Stone, a beautifully carved 1.3m neolithic artefact that may once have served as the lintel stone for a cairn, as well as the Westray Venus, a small stone fashioned into human shape, one of the oldest anthropomorphic models yet found in the British Isles. You should also check out the huge whale skeleton (on display in the garden), and you probably won't want to miss the photo of the Queen laughing when the Duke of Edinburgh banged his head getting into the bus on the royal visit to Westray in 1960.

Lady Kirk

MAP PAGE 82
Pierowall, Westray, KW17 2DG
ⓦ historicenvironment.scot/visit-a-place/ places/pierowall-church. Open 24hr. Free.

Fenced off for safety inspections and possible renovation at time of research, **Lady Kirk** in Pierowall dates back to the 1200s, though much of the extant church dates from the seventeenth century. It contains a set of 'grave-slabs', intricately designed stones set into the wall in memory of some of the village's higher-status inhabitants.

Quoygrew

MAP PAGE 82
Rackwick Rd, Westray, KW17 2DN.
Open 24hr. Free.

The remains of a thirteenth-century farmhouse are still evident at the remote site of **Quoygrew** on Westray's northwest coast. Archeologists have determined that a Scandinavian fishing community was established here in about 950 AD, but the focus shifted to farming at some point from 1200 onwards. The site was still inhabited as late as the 1930s: the ruins of the croft from this more modern age can be seen just up the slope.

Noltland Castle

MAP PAGE 82
Westray, KW17 2DW ⓦ historicenvironment. scot/visit-a-place/places/noltland-castle.
April–Sept 9.30am–5.30pm; Oct–March 10am–4pm. Free.

The home of the sixteenth-century Sir Gilbert Balfour, generally acknowledged as a bit of a bad 'un, is found about half a mile to the west of Pierowall, in a commanding spot overlooking

Reaching Papa Westray

Papa Westray is famous as the destination of the world's shortest scheduled flight: the journey lasts approximately two minutes. You'll need to book this in advance, as it only runs roughly twice a week from Westray and does sell out. Other options for getting to Papa Westray include the foot passenger ferry from Pierowall, which takes about 25 minutes and leaves multiple times daily, or the twice-weekly car ferry from Kirkwall, which takes about one hour and 30 minutes.

the coast and surrounding hills. Balfour had a chequered career, his fortunes waxing and waning with those of Mary, Queen of Scots, and after her downfall he retreated first here to Orkney and thereafter to Sweden, where he was subsequently executed for plotting the death of the King of Sweden.

Noltland Castle is a rather dour and forbidding place: the enormous kitchen with its domed ceiling is dark and atmospherically creepy, while the outsized spiral staircase leading to the upper floor speaks to Balfour's delusions of grandeur. The apparently excessive number of gun holes in the exterior wall suggests that Balfour was not a universally popular chap.

Climb to the top of the tower for views across Westray.

Grobust Beach and the Links of Noltland

MAP PAGE 82
Westray, KW7 2DW Ⓦ historicenvironment. scot/visit-a-place/places/links-of-noltland. Open 24hr. Free.

Westray punches above its weight when it comes to pretty beaches,

Noup Head Lighthouse

but undoubtedly one of its best is **Grobust**, unfurling to the northwest of Pierowall. The bay is impossibly idyllic, with a gorgeous sweep of white sand occasionally punctuated by smears of black sand, lending the beach's beauty a subtle complexity. An outcrop of layered flat black rock runs down the centre of the beach, offering a perfect place to sit and watch the tide come in as the sun sets.

This area is also notable for its prehistoric archeology: behind the beach is a wave of grassy sand dunes concealing the **Links of Noltland**, a neolithic farming settlement. It's here that many significant finds have been unearthed, including a small neolithic figurine known as the Westray Wife (or the Orkney Venus). Also in the vicinity, along a short path to the beach's west, is the Knowe of Queen o'Howe, a grassy mound that's thought to be an unexcavated broch.

Noup Head Lighthouse

MAP PAGE 82
Westray, KW17 2DW Ⓦ nlb.org.uk/lighthouses/noup-head. Open 24hr. Free.

Found in a dramatic position atop towering cliffs on Westray's northwest tip, **Noup Head Lighthouse** was designed and built by David Stevenson in the late nineteenth century. You can't access the inside of the lighthouse, but it makes a perfect destination for a coastal walk (see box, opposite). Alternatively, it is possible to drive to the lighthouse, but it's a pretty bumpy road.

Papa Westray

A small island off the northeast coast of Westray, **Papa Westray** – often referred to as Papay – has a lot to offer, boasting one of Orkney's archeological powerhouses. It's also home to an excellent ethnographic museum and some fine coastal scenery,

Walk to Noup Head Lighthouse

The two- to three-hour walk begins from the small parking area at Backaras, where you start by following the path downhill between two fields. Cross a stile at the bottom, then hop over another stile to turn right. (The sign here points left, but this is only recommended if you want to circumnavigate the entirety of Westray.) Trace the cliff edge, taking in the scenic coastal vistas as you go; don't miss the impressive rock arches here.

Clamber over a further two stiles into a field; at this point, the path becomes a little indistinct, but keep the sea quite close on your left and you won't go wrong. As you reach the top of a rise, you should see a footpath sign in the middle of the field – once you're past that, the way becomes obvious again. Cross a small brook and then another stile, before veering off to the cliff edge to enjoy some gorgeously elemental coastline and – if you're here on a summer's evening – hundreds of nesting puffins.

Follow the track that skirts the left of the hill, ascending gently: eventually, you'll turn a corner and the lighthouse will come into view, poking out from behind a curious promontory that vaguely resembles books stacked on top of one another.

Pass through a gate and continue along the path, curving around the small and oddly named Loch of the Stack. Climb the promontory – at the top of the first platform, don't forget to look back, as the cliffs here are another puffin hotspot in summer, and in any case are stunning whenever you're here.

Continue the ascent, following any of the rough tracks until you reach the trig point. There are great views of the lighthouse from here, but the vista is even better if you descend slightly and head towards the cliff edge – the lighthouse, poised right on the tip of these vertiginous cliffs, makes a beautiful sight.

Now, you need to head back – either retrace your footsteps, or head past the lighthouse on its right-hand side to pick up an unpaved road that you can follow back to the parking area. The road route is a little quicker but considerably less interesting. Whichever you opt for, the entire walk should take you between two and three hours.

Two notes of caution: firstly, the cliffs are sheer, so take great care around them, and consider weather conditions before setting out. If it's windy or foggy, this hike is not a great idea. Secondly, nesting seabirds can be aggressive if you stray too close to their nests: give them a wide berth.

making it well worth taking the hop across from Westray.

Knap of Howar

MAP PAGE 82
Papa Westray, KW17 2BU
Ⓦ historicenvironment.scot/visit-a-place/ places/knap-of-howar. Open 24hr. Free.
The enormously significant archeological site of the **Knap of Howar** consists of two small chambers that are thought to be Northern Europe's oldest surviving stone house; built potentially as long ago as 3700 BC, it's older than Egypt's Pyramids. Probably deliberately abandoned in around 2900 BC, the Knap was covered in sand over the millennia before being

excavated in the 1930s. You can explore the two rooms and admire the still extant features, including a hearth, alcoves and interior divides.

A little way south is a more minor archeological site, the Burnt Mound. It's unlikely to rock your world and is probably only worth a visit if you're a real Papa Westray completist.

John o'Holland's Bothy Museum

MAP PAGE 82
Papa Westray, KW17 2BU. Open 24hr. Free.
This great little ethnographic **museum**, housed in the croft building once owned by local farmer John o'Holland, can be found at the top of the footpath leading down to the Knap of Howar. Inside, you'll see items that vividly illustrate what everyday life was like here during the early to mid-twentieth century, with exhibits covering fishing, working in the dairy, and leisure time. Look out for the ingenious 'moustache cup', designed so a man could drink his tea without dunking his tache. There's a small selection of handmade souvenirs on sale here, with proceeds going to charity.

St Boniface Kirk

MAP PAGE 82
Papa Westray, KW17 2BU. Open 24hr. Free.
One of the oldest churches in Orkney, **St Boniface Kirk** may have been established in the eighth century, though the present building dates from the twelfth. It fell into disuse in the twentieth century, but underwent extensive restoration in the 1990s. There's a small exhibition inside, detailing archeological finds in the surrounding area.

The Kelp Store Heritage and Arts Centre

MAP PAGE 82
Papa Westray, KW17 2BU ⓦ thekelpstore-papawestray.com. Open 24hr. Free
The Kelp Store Heritage and Art Centre, found in the former kelp store building, is a little light on exhibits but makes for a fascinating stop regardless. Films cover various aspects of island life, from the local industries of farming and fishing, through to how World War II affected Papa Westray, alongside

Knap of Howar

John o'Holland's Bothy Museum

displays on shipwrecks in nearby waters. You'll also find a decent library of local interest books, census records, and a small kitchen where you can make yourself a cup of tea.

Chapel of St Tredwell

MAP PAGE 82

Papa Westray, KW17 2BU. Open 24hr. Free.

From the T-junction at the bottom of the road from the island shop and hostel, turn right and follow a gravel track to reach the ancient **Chapel of St Tredwell**. Tredwell was a Holy Virgin with one of those macabre stories that the early Christians seemed to relish: when propositioned by the Pictish King Nechtan, who complimented her eyes, she responded by having her eyes gouged out and presented them to him. The chapel was, accordingly, long a place of pilgrimage for those suffering blindness and eye afflictions. It's almost entirely ruined now, but it's a pleasant walk to get here.

North Papa Westray

MAP PAGE 82

The **northern end** of Papa Westray is given over to the RSPB reserve of North Hill: here, you'll find some gorgeous coastal scenery, birdwatching hides, and a memorial statue to the Great Auk, a bird that once could be found on the island but was hunted to extinction in the 1800s. This statue, however, has been described as looking "nothing like a Great Auk", and in April 2022, it was announced it would be replaced with a bronze statue produced from a digital scan and 3D printing of a Great Auk specimen held by the Natural History Museum.

Holm of Papa

MAP PAGE 82

Those wishing to really get off the beaten track may want to consider a trip to the miniscule island of the **Holm of Papa**, off Papa Westray's east coast. It's home to three chambered cairns, the most interesting at the island's southern end, which contains examples of neolithic carved art.

Trips to the Holm of Papa can be arranged by contacting the Papay Development Trust in advance on ☎ 01857 644224.

Handmade knitwear from Hume Sweet Hume

Shops

Hume Sweet Hume

MAP PAGE 82

Pierowall, Westray, KW17 2BZ

Ⓦ humesweethume.co.uk. Mon–Sat 2–4pm.

This little boutique shop may sell candles, cards and jewellery too, but the star of the show is the exquisite designer knitwear, which is created from Westray wool by sisters Lizza and Jenna.

Westray Heritage Centre

MAP PAGE 82

Pierowall, Westray, KW17 2BZ

Ⓦ westrayheritage.co.uk.

Mon 11.30am–5pm, Tues–Sat 9am–noon & 2–5pm, Sun 1.30–5pm.

The gift shop attached to Westray Heritage Centre boasts a fantastic range of goods, almost all unique to the island – where else could you buy a replica of the Westray Venus or a Westray Stone tea towel? There's also a selection of lovely handicrafts, most made by local artisans.

Wheeling Steen Gallery

MAP PAGE 82

Westray, KW17 2DN Ⓦ wheeling-steen. co.uk. Mon & Wed–Sat 1–5pm.

A mile or two north of Pierowall, the *Wheeling Steen Gallery* sells artwork and photography, much of it focused on Orkney and Westray. It's worth a visit just to see the deck cabin of a nineteenth-century shipwreck, around which the gallery has been built. Another incentive is the attached small café, which dishes up frozen yoghurt to popular acclaim.

Eating on Papa Westray

At time of writing, there were no eating establishments on Papa Westray, meaning that the island shop is your only source of food while here. The shop keeps pretty short hours: Mon–Fri 9.30am–11am & 3.30–5.30pm (closed Tues afternoons), Sat 9.30am–11am & 6–7pm. It's not open at all on Sundays. Bringing a picnic to Papa Westray is therefore very much recommended.

Cafés

Jack's Chippy

MAP PAGE 82
Pierowall, Westray, KW17 2DA ⓣ 01857
677471, ⓦ pierowall-fish.co.uk/jacks.php.
Wed & Sat 4.30–7.30pm.

A takeaway fish and chips shop
in Pierowall is just the ticket on a
sunny evening. In all honesty, the
chips here are so-so – more like
fries than chip-shop chips – but the
fish is sublime: soft, succulent and
perfectly battered. It's only open on
Wednesday and Saturday evenings,
so plan accordingly. £

Richan's Retreat

MAP PAGE 82
Rapness, Westray, KW17 2DE
ⓣ 01857677877,
ⓦ aakwork.co.uk/richans-retreat.html.
Daily 8am–6.30pm.

A few hundred metres from the ferry
terminal at Rapness, *Richan's Retreat*
is a lovely little place for coffee, cake
and conversation: owners Paul and
Linda are always up for a welcoming
chat. It doubles as a craft shop too,
making it a perfect place to pick up
Westray souvenirs. £

Saintear

MAP PAGE 82
Westray, KW17 2DP
ⓣ 07825 017124, ⓦ facebook.com/
Saintear-108126354709148. Mon–Wed &
Sat 9.30am–4pm, Fri 5–6.30pm.

Just outside Pierowall with a fine
location overlooking Loch Saintear,
this friendly little bistro is one of
Westray's best lunch options. The
menu consists of a good range of
paninis, as well as daily changing
soups and quiches. Don't miss the
delicious home-made cakes for dessert
– the cinnamon swirl is excellent. ££

Pub

The Pierowall Hotel

MAP PAGE 82
Pierowall, Westray, KW17 2BZ
ⓣ 01857 677472, ⓦ pierowallhotel.co.uk.
Daily noon–2pm & 5–8pm.

This hotel on Pierowall's front is the
only place on Westray where you
can reliably get an evening meal,
so it's worth booking to ensure
they can fit you in. There's a decent
menu, including lamb tagines and
fish and chips, as well as a tempting
range of desserts. ££

Hume Sweet Hume in Pierowall

Northern isles

It's hugely worthwhile taking a trip away from Mainland to explore at least one of Orkney's outlying islands: easily accessed by ferry from Kirkwall, the northern isles – Shapinsay, Eday, Stronsay, Sanday and North Ronaldsay – reward visitors with beautiful beaches and coastal scenery, fantastic archeological remains, magnificent birdwatching opportunities, and above all, the feeling of exploration. Many travellers to Orkney don't venture beyond Mainland, but they're missing out on such treasures as Stronsay's Vat of Kirbuster, Sanday's Quoyness Chambered Cairn, Eday's Stone of Setter, and much more besides.

Shapinsay

The closest of the northern isles to Mainland, **Shapinsay** is an ideal choice for a day-trip. It boasts a pretty village with a disproportionately large Gothic castle (regrettably not open to the public), as well as some rewarding coastal walking and a very fine broch. It's large enough to warrant some form of transport; if you don't bring your car, consider arranging electric bike hire via ⓔ ebike@shapinsay.org.uk.

Balfour

MAP PAGE 94

The Shapinsay ferry arrives into **Balfour**, the island's only community of any size. Set around an attractive harbour and lined with stone-built cottages, it's undoubtedly one of Orkney's prettiest villages. The most noteworthy building here is Balfour Castle, a fairytale-like fortress that was constructed in the eighteenth century for the Balfour family, who owned much of Shapinsay between the fifteenth and twentieth centuries. The castle is sadly not open to the public, but you can see its imposing facade from the driveway, accessible from the gatehouse to the left of the harbour. The best view of it, however, is from the ferry as you arrive on or leave the island.

The Shapinsay Heritage Arts and Crafts Centre, the only other specific sight in the village, was undergoing renovation at the time of research, but hopes were high for its reopening in time for the 2023 tourist season.

Tourist information

Though none of the northern isles boasts a dedicated tourist information centre, the heritage centres on some of the islands (particularly Sanday) will be able to offer an informal tourist information service. Most islands also have a tourist information website:

Eday ⓦ visiteday.wordpress.com
Stronsay ⓦ visitstronsay.com
Sanday ⓦ visitsanday.com
North Ronaldsay ⓦ northronaldsay.co.uk

Reaching Shapinsay

There are up to six ferries daily between Kirkwall and Shapinsay, with a journey time of 25 minutes. Ferries depart from a dedicated Shapinsay terminal, on the seafront opposite the Orkney Distillery and Visitor Centre. If taking a car, you'll need to reverse on to the ferry. Note that the ramp at the Shapinsay end tilts at quite an extravagant angle, so take care when reversing on for the return trip. Ferry staff are always happy to guide you, and may offer to drive your vehicle on for you.

RSPB Mill Dam Nature Reserve

MAP PAGE 94
Shapinsay, KW17 2DY ⓦ rspb.org.uk/reserves-and-events/reserves-a-z/mill-dam. Open 24hr. Free.

In the centre of Shapinsay, the **RSPB Mill Dam Nature Reserve** is a wetlands area that provides habitat for a great variety of Orkney's birdlife. There's a hide here, from which you may see oystercatchers, peregrine falcons, and the elusive water rail, a fairly uncommon species only found at a few sites in Orkney.

Vasa Loch and Agricola

MAP PAGE 94
Further birdwatching opportunities await at the small lakes of **Vasa** and **Agricola**, on the southwest coast of the island. Here, you're most likely to see waders of various descriptions, as well as migratory Arctic terns in the summer. There are fine views across to the island of Gairsay and Orkney's Mainland, and if you fancy a longer leg stretch, it's possible to follow the coast path back to Balfour.

Burroughston Broch

MAP PAGE 94
Off B9058, Shapinsay, KW17 2EB.
Open 24hr. Free.

Arguably Shapinsay's top sight, **Burroughston Broch** at the northeast tip of the island is one of the finest to be found on Orkney. On the approach along the grassy path, it appears to be little more than a grassy mound, but once you pass beneath the lintel stone, you'll find yourself in a perfectly round ancient tower. It's possible to clearly make out the broch's features, including a well, the outlines of interior rooms, and a set of extremely neat alcoves. Beside the entrance are a couple of small rooms set in the exterior wall – one of these contains a spyhole that looks through into the exterior passage, allowing those inside to easily see who'd come calling.

Dedicated broch enthusiasts may also wish to check out the example at the Ness of Ork, about a mile away, but this is as yet unexcavated and all you'll be able to see is a

Vasa Loch

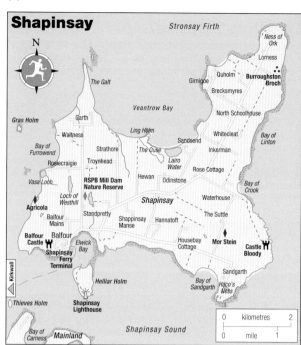

Shapinsay

Stronsay Firth

N

[Map labels, roughly north to south and west to east:]
Ness of Ork
Lorness
The Galt
Girnigoe
Quholm
Burroughston Broch
Brecksmyres
Gras Holm
Garth
Veantrow Bay
North Schoolhouse
Waltness
Ling Holm
Whitecleat
Bay of Furrowend
Strathore
Sandsend
Inkerman
Bay of Linton
Rosiecraigie
Troynhead
The Ouse
Lairo Water
Rose Cottage
Vasa Loch
Hewan
RSPB Mill Dam Nature Reserve
Odinstone
Shapinsay
Bay of Crook
Loch of Westhill
Agricola
Standpretty
Waterhouse
Balfour Mains
Balfour
Shappinsay Manse
Hannatoft
The Suttle
Kirkwall
Balfour Castle
Elwick Bay
Shapinsay Ferry Terminal
Housebay Cottage
Mor Stein
Castle Bloody
Helliar Holm
Bay of Sandgarth
Sandgarth
Haco's Ness
Shapinsay Lighthouse
Thieves Holm
Bay of Carness
Mainland
Shapinsay Sound

0 — kilometres — 2
0 — mile — 1

---

circular bank indicating where the broch's walls once were.

The southeast

MAP PAGE 94

Shapinsay's **southeast** corner offers a couple of options if you find yourself with extra time to kill while on the island. Stood beside a minor road connecting the B9058 and B9059 is the Mor Stein, a neolithic standing stone. Visible from here, and reached along a path that begins at the north end of this road, is a chambered cairn known as Castle Bloody. Neither of these can be classed as essential stops.

Eday

The eight mile-long island of **Eday** makes another good choice for a day-trip from Kirkwall, on which history buffs are especially well catered for with some excellent archeological sites, including several chambered cairns and one of Orkney's finest standing stones. It's also home to several lovely beaches and some great coastal scenery, which also offers birdwatching opportunities.

Eday Heritage & Visitor Centre

MAP PAGE 96

B9063, Eday, KW17 2AB Ⓦ facebook.com/Eday-Heritage-Centre-1809537222704597. Daily 9am–6pm. Free.

In an old church just north of the airfield, the **Eday Heritage & Visitor Centre** offers an intriguing glimpse into the island's past. Amid a slightly haphazard collection of artefacts from the twentieth century, there are good displays on farming, the two World Wars, and the peat industry. Perhaps the most interesting story here is that of the crate of whisky – distilled using Eday peat – that Shackleton took on his 1907 trip to the South

Pole and was subsequently found, one hundred years later, buried in the Antarctic ice. There are plans for the centre to receive a bit of a spruce-up in time for the 2023 tourist season: hopefully, this will involve the return of the excellent café that was once on site.

Stone of Setter

MAP PAGE 96
Off B9063, Eday, KW17 2AB.
Open 24hr. Free.

The atmospheric lichen covered **Stone of Setter** is one of Orkney's largest standing stones, and is thought to originally have been higher still. Its size may indicate that Eday was once an island of some importance. It stands alone in a field not far from the island's shop, and is the first stop on the Eday Heritage Walk. Just south of the Stone is Mill Loch, a great spot for birdwatchers to catch sight of many species, most importantly red-throated divers, which are found here in one of the UK's densest breeding populations. There's a hide here that contains some helpful info boards about what birdlife you're likely to see.

Braeside, Huntersquoy and Vinquoy tombs

MAP PAGE 96
Off B9063, Eday, KW17 2AB.
Open 24hr. Free.

A set of small archeological sites lies just a short distance from the Stone of Setter – follow the Eday Heritage Walk (see box, page 97) to first reach **Braeside Chambered Cairn**, which is aligned directly with the Stone of Setter. A short

Eday Heritage & Visitor Centre

stroll further on is **Huntersquoy Chambered Cairn**, which once contained two chambers: only one of these is still extant and it's usually flooded, so you probably won't be able to enter.

The third tomb, **Vinquoy Chambered Cairn**, is now visible on the crest of the hill ahead. Don't be fooled by what appears to be a massive set of earthworks ahead of you: this is a modern construction, intended to conceal a water tank, and not doing a terribly good job of it from some angles. Instead, bear to the right where the genuine cairn awaits. It can be entered, though you'll need to bend double and use a torch. From the large internal room, you'll see four smaller chambers off to the sides.

Reaching Eday

There are two ferries a day to Eday from Kirkwall, some of which call at Sanday or Stronsay en route. If the trip is direct, it takes one hour and 15 minutes, but can be twice that if the ferry is going via one of the other islands. Loganair operates weekly flights to Eday's airport (known as London Airport) on Wednesdays: these get booked up, so make sure you book well in advance.

NORTHERN ISLES

Isthmus beaches

MAP PAGE 96
Off B9063, Eday, KW17 2AA.
Open 24hr. Free.

Separated from one another by a small rocky outcrop, backed by grassy dunes, and characterized by beautiful fine white sand, the **Sands of Mussetter** and **Doomy** are a pair of lovely long **beaches** that you're likely to have to yourself even on a sunny day at the height of the tourist season. Access to both is from a little parking area at the west end of Mussetter.

Bay of London

MAP PAGE 96
B9063, Eday, KW17 2AA. Open 24hr. Free.

Just across the road from Eday's airfield, the pleasant if unremarkable stretch of sand is perhaps worth a visit simply so you can confuse people by telling them that while on Orkney you went to the **beach** at London Airport. If

such silliness doesn't appeal, you'll probably be better served by Eday's other beaches such as the Sands of Mussetter.

Kirk Tang

MAP PAGE 96
Off B9063, Eday, KW17 2AA.
Open 24hr. Free.

If you find yourself at a loose end, consider making a short visit to **Kirk Tang**, an atmospheric ruined church poised in an attractive spot on the east coast. Though not an island highlight, it's worth a quick stop.

The south coast

MAP PAGE 96
Off B9063, Eday, KW17 2AA.
Open 24hr. Free.

Sights along Eday's **south coast** are more limited, though there is a decent circular walk that heads along the shoreline, past the very scanty ruins of an old church known as Hannah's Kirk, then up

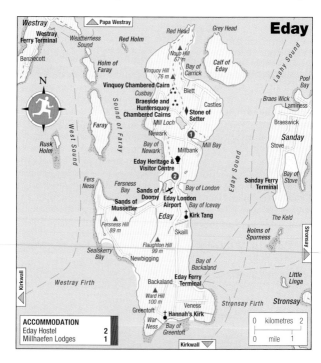

Eday Heritage Walk

A reasonably well-marked and easily navigable trail of about six miles leads around the top sights of Eday's northwest corner. Starting with the Stone of Setter, you can follow the trail to Vinquoy Chambered Cairn (see page 95), Noup Hill and Carrick House, where the pirate John Gow was held prisoner before his transfer to London for execution (see box, page 39), among much else. There's a map detailing the route at Mill Loch (see page 95), and another at the Eday Heritage & Visitor Centre (see page 94), but there are no leaflets to take away, so it would be sensible to take a photo of one of these maps before setting off. The return section of the walk from Carrick House back to the island shop, where you'll probably park, is a bit of a tedious slog, so you may wish to consider returning the way you came after looping round Noup Hill headland. The route sometimes involves boardwalks but is more often on paths that are liable to be boggy, so be sure to wear sensible footwear.

to Eday's highest point, the summit of Ward Hill, from which you'll get good views across the neighbouring islands. Return via paths leading past Greentoft Farm, which dates back to the sixteenth century. Very limited parking for this walk can be found at the T-junction where the road from *Roadside B&B* becomes an unsurfaced track.

Stronsay

The vaguely star-shaped island of **Stronsay** is plaited with beautiful sandy beaches, a healthy home-grown crafts tradition (see box, page 100), and one of Orkney's finest natural sights: the **Vat of Kirbuster** (see page 99), a marvellous rock arch that forms the centrepiece of a lovely clifftop walk. If you only have time to visit one of the northern isles, Stronsay is a strong choice.

Whitehall

MAP PAGE 98

Stronsay's main settlement, **Whitehall**, is an attractive little village that's well set up with facilities, boasting a café and a decent shop, which – among much else – offers the loan of electric bikes free of charge. The heritage

centre is found here too, as is the only accommodation available on the island. The main street is a pretty place for a quick wander, and you can extend your stroll a short way south from the village to reach a small but attractive beach called the Ayre of the Myres.

Stronsay Heritage Centre

MAP PAGE 98

Wood's Yard, Whitehall, Stronsay, KW17 2AR. 9am–6pm. Free.

The **Stronsay Heritage Centre** – at time of writing tucked away in temporary premises in a yard at the west end of Whitehall, but expected to move to a new building nearer the pier at some undetermined point – contains a motley collection of artefacts from the island's past, with a certain emphasis on the fishing industry that was once prevalent here. There's an admirable hands-on approach here: most excitingly, you're invited to activate the island's World War II air-raid siren by turning its handle.

The isthmus beaches

MAP PAGE 98

On either side of Stronsay's narrow neck, you'll find a gorgeous beach.

The Calf of Eday

If walking to Noup Hill (see page 97), look east to see the small uninhabited island of the Calf of Eday. The rocky speck is home to a neolithic chambered cairn, but perhaps its greatest claim to fame is the moment in February 1725 when the pirate John Gow ran aground here and was captured. Events on the island are generally less dramatic these days, but it has been designated a Special Protection Area ifor its great variety of seabirds.

St Catherine's Bay, on the west, is simply stunning, with white sand as fine and soft as dust, backed by grassy dunes and spread along a wide bay with views across to several of Orkney's other islands. It's accessible down a track from the main road to a parking area: this track is quite rough, but can be negotiated.

The east side of the isthmus is sculpted by **Mill Bay**, which is similarly sandy, dune-backed and pretty, and enjoys a couple of folkloric traditions too – the Well of Kildinguie, for instance, allegedly has the power to cure all diseases except the Black Death. Though its location seems to have been known well enough in centuries past, it's now nigh on impossible to find the well.

To reach the beach, turn off the main road opposite the fire station, and park near the now-derelict mill. On the other side of the road, a path (signed "no dumping" rather than anything helpful like "beach") leads down to the sands.

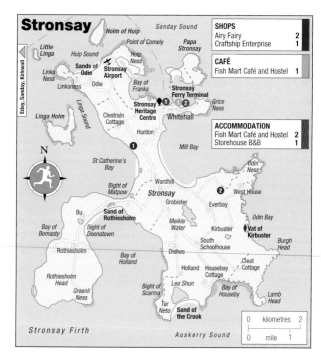

SHOPS	
Airy Fairy	2
Craftship Enterprise	1

CAFÉ	
Fish Mart Café and Hostel	1

ACCOMMODATION	
Fish Mart Café and Hostel	2
Storehouse B&B	1

Vat of Kirbuster

Of the two, St Catherine's is probably the prettier, though Mill Bay is easier to access, despite not being signposted.

Vat of Kirbuster

MAP PAGE 98
KW17 2AG. Open 24hr. Free.

Stronsay's premier attraction, the **Vat of Kirbuster**, is a muscular rock arch found in the rugged cliffs on the island's east coast. It's an excellent demonstration of the power of the forces of nature, particularly on a stormy day, when the waves crash through the Vat dramatically.

To reach it, park in the layby signposted as the beginning of the Vat of Kirbuster walk. Follow the signpost through the gates to the coast, where another sign directs you to turn right and walk along the cliff edge. The scenery here is attractively wild and rugged, and the sound of the sea battering the cliffs provides an excellent soundtrack to your walk. There's also plenty of opportunity for birdwatching on this route, with seabirds including fulmars and guillemots all nesting in the cliffs. It's a matter of only five to ten minutes' walk before you reach the Vat.

It's well worth continuing at least a little way along the path: shortly after the Vat, the trail passes by a pair of sea stacks, then meanders its way along the coast to Burgh Head past further marvellously elemental scenery.

From Burgh Head, you'll catch a glimpse of Lamb Head, a peninsula replete with yet more serene views of beautiful cliffs (to which the path continues). If you hike as far as Lamb Head, it's

Reaching Stronsay

There up are to three ferries daily from Kirkwall to Stronsay, taking about one hour and 40 minutes if direct, or just over two hours via Eday. Flights from Kirkwall to Stronsay, taking a total of nine minutes, run daily (except Sundays).

Stronsay Craft Trail

Craft shops are common across Orkney, but there's a particular concentration of them in Stronsay, to the extent that there's a dedicated Stronsay Craft Trail. Starting at the *Craftship Enterprise*, housed in a former chapel on the island's west coast, you can visit a string of artisanal shops selling home-made products, from jewellery and glass to soap and textiles.

possible to make this a circular walk, but as much of the return route is along minor roads and isn't hugely exciting, you may prefer to walk back the same way you came.

The south

MAP PAGE 98
Off B9060, Stronsay, KW17 2AJ.
Open 24hr. Free.
Birdwatchers may enjoy a visit to the hide at the small lake of Lea Shun, reached via a path from the graveyard at the end of a small road off the B9060. If you're desperate for a beach even more isolated than Stronsay's other offerings, consider walking around the **southern coast** from the graveyard to the small Sand of the Crook.

The Stronsay coast is best explored on foot

Rothiesholm

MAP PAGE 98
Rothiesholm, Stronsay, KW17 2AN.
Open 24hr. Free.
Orkney has more than its fair share of beautiful beaches, making choosing between them difficult: if you're unsure which sandy swathe to head for, **Rothiesholm** is a very strong contender. Its turquoise waters and white sands are gorgeous, the sea is calm and safe (if cold) for swimmers, and it's also an excellent spot for shell seeking. If this beach were in Devon or Cornwall, say, it would be packed out all summer long: here, the car park, which has space for about four cars, is rarely occupied.

A circular walk starts here, taking in the beach and heading north to the other side of the headland and along. En route, you'll pass by the Hillock of Baywest, an ancient burial mound that has yet to be excavated.

Papa Stronsay

MAP PAGE 98
From Whitehall village, you'll be able to see **Papa Stronsay**, a small island off Stronsay's northeast coast. It's home to an active community of monks, and can be visited if you contact the monastery via their website (Ⓦ papastronsay.com/index. php) to arrange transport. While on the island, you can explore the ruins of St Nicholas' Chapel, which date from the eleventh century, and visit the chambered cairn of Earl's Knowle.

Sanday

Sanday's tourism slogan proclaims that "there's nothing to do on

Pow Bay, Stronsay

Sanday", but this is clearly tongue-in-cheek, as **Sanday** is in fact blessed with a huge variety of things to see and do. As its name suggests, this is a sandy island, and as such there are some of Orkney's finest beaches here, but it's also home to excellent archeological remains, some fine wartime heritage, and one of the best museums on Orkney. Spending a couple of days here is well worth the trip.

The southwest

MAP PAGE 102

If arriving by ferry, you'll begin your exploration of Sanday on a small finger of land that points **southwest** towards Eday. This peninsula is scattered with several archeological sites and fringed by a couple of fine beaches.

Archeology-wise, on the west coast, the small bay of **Pool** was a productive dig site in the 1990s, while the **Ness of Brough** yielded Viking graves during a Time Team exploration. They're both reasonably attractive places to stop, but unless you're an expert, there's little in particular to see, so you may prefer to opt for one of Sanday's famously showstopping beaches.

One such is **Doun Helzie**, which can be reached by a waymarked path that starts at the farm track just north of the electricity substation on the road down to Stove. Note that this route involves walking along cliff edges and descending to the beach by scrambling down a dune, so you may prefer to head for **Backaskaill Bay**, a gorgeous wide beach with rolling surf and soft white sand, which is accessible via a steep but well-paved road from a small parking area.

Quoyness Chambered Cairn

MAP PAGE 102
Elsness, Sanday, KW17 2BL
ⓦ historicenvironment.scot/visit-a-place/places/quoyness-chambered-cairn.
Open 24hr. Free.

One of Orkney's top archeological sites can be found at the tip of a spit of land that protrudes from Sanday's south coast. The **Quoyness Chambered Cairn** is a perfect neolithic tomb, set in a peaceful spot by the sea. You can enter the cairn by the low passageway: once in the interior chamber, it's surprisingly light and you can peer into all the surrounding smaller rooms.

To reach the cairn, take the signposted road from the cemetery south of Lady village. Drive along the potholed and sandy but not particularly challenging road (past a grassy area that looks like it's a parking area but isn't) until you reach a marked car park. From here, walk along the sandy track, following the labelled footpath when it veers left, and then taking the obvious route to the cairn.

Lady Kirk

MAP PAGE 102
B9069, Sanday, KW17 2BL. Open 24hr. Free.
The ruins of **Lady Kirk** stand a couple of hundred metres from the access road to the Quoyness Chambered Cairn as you head towards Kettletoft. Situated in a fine position overlooking a beach, the

evocative remains are notable for the Devil's Clawmarks, a set of deep grooves in the surface of a wall at the top of the side staircase. Story has it that these were left by the Devil, who was thwarted in his attempts to drag an adulterous priest to hell. A less imaginative, if more likely, explanation is that the grooves are the result of erosion.

Sanday Heritage Centre

MAP PAGE 102
Lady Village, Sanday, KW17 2BW
ⓦ sandaydt.org. 9.30am–5pm. Free.
This extremely well set-out **museum** boasts an excellent collection exploring Sanday's past. There's a great section on the shipwrecks that can be found in the surrounding waters, including artefacts recovered from the sunken vessels and information boards on some of the more prominent examples. You'll also find a small natural history collection, and an exhibition on

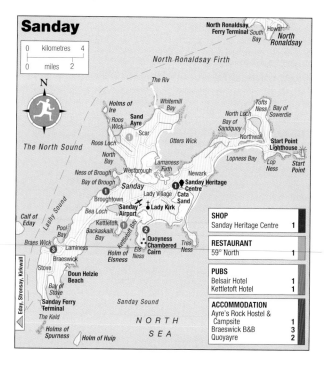

SHOP	
Sanday Heritage Centre	1

RESTAURANT	
59° North	1

PUBS	
Belsair Hotel	1
Kettletoft Hotel	1

ACCOMMODATION	
Ayre's Rock Hostel & Campsite	1
Braeswick B&B	3
Quoyayre	2

Sanday's farming heritage, but the jewel in the museum's crown is the Appiehouse Stone, a Pictish carved stone that is evidence of early Christianity on Sanday. Also, don't miss the fine Viking rune stone.

Outside, there's a life-sized replica of **Meur Burnt Mound** (see box, below), which in all honesty is more interesting than the actual site. In the corner of the field is a fantastically evocative nineteenth-century croft house; look out for the traditional Orcadian chairs among the fascinating artefacts.

Cata Sand

MAP PAGE 102
B9069, Sanday, KW17 2BW. Open 24hr. Free.
If anywhere justifies Sanday's name, it's **Cata Sand**, an immense flat bay that forms a simply enormous, long beach at low tide – so long that you can't even see the sea from the beach's top. At high tide, meanwhile, the water is beautifully shallow and turquoise – on a sunny day, it's gorgeous. On the road by the beach stands the Brickie Hut, a World War II relic that has been tipped for tourist development, though plans have as yet come to nothing, and it's currently used as a home for nesting birds. From here, you can embark on a walk along the beach or the dunes down to Tresness Cairn and Wasso Broch, a pair of archeological sites in a beautiful setting.

Lopness Bay

MAP PAGE 102
B9069, Sanday, KW17 2BP. Open 24hr. Free.
A typically Sanday beach with white sand and teal waters, backed

Sanday Heritage Centre

by pebble shingle and dunes, **Lopness Bay** is afforded extra character by the foundered wreck of the *B98*, a German World War I ship that escaped the general scuttling at Scapa Flow but ended up stranded here in 1920. At low tide, you can walk up to the wreck, and it's usually visible poking above the waves even at high tide.

As you head east along the B9059 to the Lopness Bay parking area, keep your eyes peeled for a pair of distinctive sculptures by the side of the road: C-3PO and R2-D2 are here to greet you, along with Wally the Sanday Walrus driving a car. Made with metal from scrap cars, they may not be the droids you were looking for, but they're certainly an entertaining distraction.

Burnt mounds

Found in many locations across Orkney, burnt mounds are thought to have been created over long periods of time when neolithic people heated rocks over fire, then dropped the hot stones into water to warm it. The rocks, often broken by the heat, were left piled up in these mounds. It's not known exactly why this was done, though numerous explanations, including use in cooking and bathing, have been put forward by archeologists.

Start Point Lighthouse

MAP PAGE 102
Off B9069, Sanday, KW17 2BP.
Open 24hr. Free.

Designed by Robert Stevenson, the **Start Point Lighthouse** is a distinctive beast, painted with black and white vertical stripes rather than the more usual horizontal. There's a small car park from which you can walk to it: walk up the sandy road from the car park for a very short way, and then veer left along the grass track to pass left of the wind turbine. Reaching the lighthouse is tide-dependent, so make sure you know the tide times before setting off.

Tofts Ness

MAP PAGE 102

Tofts Ness, the northeast peninsula of Sanday, is an archeological heavyweight, with scholars believing that there may be hundreds of prehistoric burial sites peppered across the landscape. That said, this pre-eminence is not particularly apparent to the untrained eye: the most obvious historical remains here are in fact a set of World War II ruins at a small settlement called Lettan, and even the most prominent prehistoric site, the Meur Burnt Mound (see box, page 103), isn't that easy to spot. You'll find it opposite a house called Meur, about halfway along the road running up the west side of Tofts Ness. Birdwatchers may get more from a visit to this corner of Sanday: a couple of small lochs provide an ideal habitat for a profusion of birdlife.

Sand Ayre

MAP PAGE 102
B9068, Sanday, KW17 2AZ. Open 24hr. Free.

Sand Ayre, at the northern tip of Sanday, is home to a couple of minor sights that are worth a quick

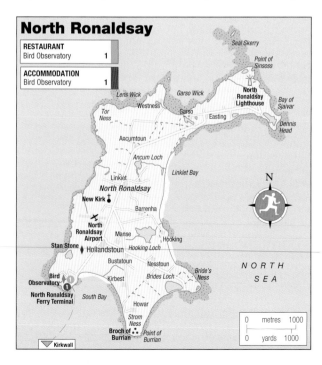

North Ronaldsay

RESTAURANT	
Bird Observatory	1

ACCOMMODATION	
Bird Observatory	1

Seal Skerry
Point of Sinsoss
Lens Wick
Garso Wick
North Ronaldsay Lighthouse
Bay of Sjaivar
Westness
Garso
Easting
Tor Ness
Dennis Head
Ancumtoun
Ancum Loch
Linklet
Linklet Bay
North Ronaldsay
New Kirk
Barrenha
North Ronaldsay Airport
Manse
Hooking
Stan Stone
Hollandstoun
Hooking Loch
Bustatoun
Nesstoun
Bride's Ness
NORTH SEA
Bird Observatory
Kirbest
Brides Loch
North Ronaldsay Ferry Terminal
South Bay
Howar
Strom Ness
Broch of Burrian
Point of Burrian
Kirkwall

N

0	metres	1000
0	yards	1000

Whitemill Bay

look if you've got time to spare. From the cemetery at the north end of the B9058, you can see the austere Scar House, a former laird's abode that now lies empty. In the far right of the field to the south of the cemetery, you can see Scar Stone, which folklore claims was thrown here from Eday by a witch.

If you head north along the road and round the corner to the left, you'll come to a farmyard where the road ends: head through this and follow the sandy track until you're above the beach. This is Sand Ayre, which was the centre of an archeological flurry in 1991 when a Viking boat burial was discovered here. The finds, which include a marvellous carved whalebone plaque, have now all been removed and are on display at Kirkwall's Orkney Museum.

Whitemill Bay

MAP PAGE 102
Off B9068, Sanday, KW17 2AZ.
Open 24hr. Free.

Another of Sanday's stunning beaches, **Whitemill Bay** is a long ribbon of fine white sand with perfect aquamarine water that sparkles in the afternoon sunlight. It's an idyllic place for a long stroll enjoying the sound of the surf. Access is via a very long road that seems to go on forever until finally reaching a small parking area.

North Ronaldsay

Orkney's northernmost island, the principal reason to visit **North Ronaldsay** is for birdwatching: as

Reaching North Ronaldsay

It is possible to get to North Ronaldsay by ferry from both Kirkwall and Papa Westray, but timings tend to be inconvenient, leaving you with the choice of spending either 25 minutes or three days on the island. If you'd prefer to visit just for the day, you're better placed taking one of Loganair's flights from Kirkwall, which take about 20 minutes and depart up to three times daily.

North Ronaldsay's seaweed-eating sheep

an important stop on migratory routes, the island is alive with an abundance of birdlife. Birdwatching isn't all North Ronaldsay has to offer, though: there is a couple of interesting archeological sites, the UK's tallest land-based lighthouse, a lovely beach or two, and some of the most unusual sheep in the world (see box, opposite).

Bird Observatory

MAP PAGE 104
Twingness, North Ronaldsay, KW17 2BE
nrbo.org.uk. Daily 11am–4pm. Free.
In the island's southwest corner, the **Bird Observatory** is worth a visit to get the lowdown on what birdlife can currently be found on North Ronaldsay. The friendly staff can arrange walking birding tours with the wardens, but make sure to contact them in advance.

South Bay

MAP PAGE 104
Twingness, North Ronaldsay, KW17 2BE.
Open 24hr. Free.
True to its name, **South Bay** hugs the southern coast of North Ronaldsay. It's a large sandy beach,

where you stand a good chance of seeing a wide variety of birdlife and seals. At the eastern end is the Broch of Burrian, which can't be ranked among Orkney's top brochs, but is worth a visit if you have time to spare.

Stan Stone

MAP PAGE 104
North Ronaldsay, KW17 2BE.
Open 24hr. Free.
North Ronaldsay's contribution to Orkney's collection of standing stones is the **Stan Stone**, which you'll find in a field just north of the Bird Observatory. It's tall and wide but very flat, and there's a circular hole bored through it about halfway up, the purpose of which remains a subject of fierce debate.

New Kirk

MAP PAGE 104
North Ronaldsay, KW17 2BE.
Daily 9am–6pm. Free.
North Ronaldsay's heritage centre is found in **New Kirk**, a few minutes' walk north of the airport. There's a good number of old photos of island life on display, and plenty of information on topics as diverse as sheep (see box, page 107), the World Wars, lighthouses and agriculture.

North Ronaldsay Lighthouse

MAP PAGE 104
Dennis Ness, North Ronaldsay KW17 2BG 07703 112224, nlb.org.uk/lighthouses/north-ronaldsay. Access by prearranged tour only. Charge.
While on the island, don't miss the chance to take a tour of the red-and-white striped **North Ronaldsay Lighthouse**. The brainchild of lighthouse designer Robert Stevenson and built in 1854, it's the tallest land-based lighthouse in the UK. After a run-through of its history and operation by Billy, the lighthouse keeper, you'll ascend the long

North Ronaldsay's sheep

One thing you'll notice on the island is the drystone wall which stretches right around its perimeter. One of the longest such walls in the world, it's here to keep the sheep on the beaches rather than on the island's interior. And why would you want the sheep on the beaches? Because they eat seaweed, of course. Confused yet?

In actual fact, the wall was erected in the 1800s to protect the island's crofts from the sheep, leaving them with no choice other than to eat seaweed. With the exception of the marine iguana of the Galapagos Islands, it's thought that North Ronaldsay's sheep are the only land animal to subsist on seaweed. The diet has made them more susceptible to copper poisoning, meaning that eating grass is now toxic for them. Although now considered at risk of extinction, farming of the sheep is carefully managed.

spiral staircase to the lamp room. Although the lighthouse is now automated, all the mechanisms here are the originals from nearly two hundred years ago, including the highly polished lenses that refract the light into hundreds of tiny rainbows.

Views from the upper chamber are impressive, stretching as far as Fair Isle – about 50km away, directly in between Orkney and Shetland – on a clear day.

Not far away, you'll see another tower, covered in scaffolding. Looking a bit diminutive in comparison, this is the older lighthouse, built in the eighteenth century but replaced when it was found that its beam was inadvertently luring ships onto the rocks rather than warning them away.

The scaffolding was put up in the early 2000s as part of an abortive plan to restore the lighthouse.

North Ronaldsay Lighthouse

NORTHERN ISLES

Shops

Airy Fairy

MAP PAGE 98
Airy Farm, Stronsay, KW17 2AG
☏ 01857 616231, ⓦ airyfairyonline.co.uk.
No set hours.

The friendly Hazel of *Airy Fairy* specializes in sewing and fabric artisanship, mostly producing unique clothes and personalized blankets for children, but also selling some attractive souvenirs such as bags and notebooks. There's also lovely artwork by her daughter on sale, and Hazel herself is a fount of Stronsay knowledge. Coffee and tea available too.

Craftship Enterprise

MAP PAGE 98
B9060, Stronsay, KW17 2AE
☏ 07785 111126, ⓦ facebook.com/craftshipenterprise. No set hours.

Craftship Enterprise is at the forefront of the Stronsay Craft Trail (see page 100), producing beautiful home-made items including knitwear, cross-stitch and much more. It keeps irregular hours, so it's best to call ahead if you want to

Thomas Sinclair's shop, Shapinsay

visit the shop; week-long crafting retreats can also be arranged.

Sanday Heritage Centre

MAP PAGE 102
Lady Village, Sanday, KW17 2BW ☏ 01857 600724, ⓦ sandaydt.org. 9.30am–5pm.

A great little shop attached to the Sanday Heritage Centre sells a lovely collection of souvenirs, including coasters, mugs and cards. You can also pick up a woolly walrus, in honour of Wally, the Arctic walrus who visited Sanday in 2018. There's a small but decent range of local interest books too.

Restaurants

59° North

MAP PAGE 102
Off B9068, Sanday, KW17 2AZ ☏ 01857 600260, ⓦ 59-degreesnorth.co.uk. Mon–Fri 9.30am–3pm, Thurs & Fri 5–8pm.

This great place proudly proclaims it serves up the UK's most northerly wood-fired pizza, and it does so in style, with a handful of tables in an airy conservatory-like room with an open kitchen. It's the sort of place you might expect to find in Brighton, so it comes as a (very welcome) surprise to come across it here on Sanday. The pizza is excellent – the Hot Honey, with spicy salami and chilli-infused honey is particularly recommended, and if you fancy something a bit different, try the banoffee pizza for dessert. There's a shop too, selling Sanday-specific souvenirs such as tea towels, mugs and bags. ££

Bird Observatory

MAP PAGE 104
Twingness, North Ronaldsay, KW17 2BE
☏ 01857 633200, ⓦ nrbo.org.uk. No set hours, but as a guide, generally noon–2pm & 5–9pm.

The café at North Ronaldsay's Bird Observatory is the best place to sample the island's famous sheep – the roast mutton dinner, with tatties, vegetables and gravy is highly recommended. Other options include local crab sandwiches, fish and chips, and an array of toasties. It's a licensed bar, and is the most happening spot on the island in the evenings. ££

Café

Fish Mart Café and Hostel

MAP PAGE 98
Whitehall, Stronsay, KW17 2AR
☎ 01857 616401, ⓦ stronsaycafehostel.
weebly.com. April–Sept Tues–Fri 7am–3pm,
Sat 9am–2pm, Sun 11am–2.30pm; Oct–
March Wed–Fri 7am–2pm, Sat 9am–2pm,
Sun 11am–2.30pm.
A most welcome spot just round the corner from the ferry terminal, the *Fish Mart Café* is perfect for full Scottish breakfasts on arrival, or an easy lunch involving a panini, burger or baked potato. There's also an absolutely fantastic selection of home-made cakes: the chocolate fudge is highly recommended. £

Pubs

Belsair Hotel

MAP PAGE 102
Kettletoft, Sanday, KW17 2BJ
☎ 01857 600206, ⓦ facebook.com/
belsairhotel. Tues & Thurs noon–3pm, Fri
& Sat 4pm–midnight.
Just next to Kettletoft's small harbour, the *Belsair* is a smart pub that offers sandwiches, toasties

The North Ronaldsay Bird Observatory has a restaurant and guesthouse

and burgers at lunchtime, and a wider menu of pub classics in the evening. Try to leave room for one of its indulgent sundaes. ££

Kettletoft Hotel

MAP PAGE 102
Kettletoft, Sanday, KW17 2BJ
☎ 01857 600217. Mon, Tues & Fri noon–
2pm, Tues also 5–8pm, Fri also 5pm–1am,
Wed 3pm–midnight, Thurs 5pm–midnight,
Sat noon–1am, Sun noon–5pm.
Next door to the *Belsair*, the *Kettletoft* is open on Wednesday evenings for fish and chips and on Sundays for carvery roasts. ££

Eating on Shapinsay and Eday

Note that at time of writing, there were no cafés or restaurants on Shapinsay, though when the Heritage Centre reopens, there should be an attached tearoom. The best place currently to get food is at *Thomas Sinclair's*, the general store in Balfour, which can sometimes rustle up fresh sandwiches, though this can't be relied on. It may be advisable to bring a picnic from Mainland.

Similarly, there is nowhere to eat on Eday, though you can get a coffee or tea at the Eday Heritage Centre (see page 94; donation requested). The island shop is very well stocked, so it's always possible to put together a picnic.

ACCOMMODATION

Wild camping on Rackwick Beach, Hoy

Accommodation

Orkney offers a great range of accommodation, with a widespread selection of hotels, B&Bs, hostels and self-catering digs. The best choice of places to stay is found on Mainland, especially in Kirkwall, where you'll rarely have trouble finding somewhere to sleep; West Mainland and Stromness also have a decent range of options. Elsewhere, Westray, Sanday and Hoy have a reasonable number of places to stay, while Stronsay, Eday and Rousay are rather more limited, and Shapinsay has no accommodation at all. By and large, rates on Orkney's Mainland are noticeably higher than on the islands. Self-catering pads tend to require a minimum stay of at least three nights and sometimes a week, though this is often negotiable in low season. If you have the equipment for it, wild camping or overnighting in your motorhome is always an option, though be aware that you must comply with the Scottish Outdoor Access Code (ⓦoutdooraccess-scotland.scot).

Stromness and around

BRINKIES GUEST HOUSE MAP PAGE 28. Brownstown Rd, Stromness, KW16 3JN ⓣ 01856 851881, ⓦ facebook.com/BrinkiesBraeStromness. This B&B in the countryside just outside Stromness is a lovely relaxing spot, offering excellent views across town and to the islands beyond. Yvonne is a very friendly host, rooms are comfortable, the breakfasts splendid, and children will love the resident goats. ££

BURNSIDE FARM BED & BREAKFAST MAP PAGE 28. North End Rd, Stromness KW16 3LJ ⓣ 01856 850723, ⓦ burnside-farm.com. On a former dairy farm a short walk from Stromness, *Burnside Farm* is a friendly B&B with stylish and comfortable rooms. Joy and Robbie are excellent hosts with a wealth of local knowledge to help you plan your trip, and they also supply a very fine breakfast. ££

FERRY INN MAP PAGE 26. 10 John St, Stromness, KW16 3AD ⓣ 01856 850280,

Accommodation price codes

Each accommodation reviewed in this Guide is accompanied by a price category, based on the cost of a standard double room for two people in high season. Price ranges include breakfast, unless stated otherwise.

£	under £75
££	£75–£110
£££	over £110

W **ferryinn.com**. The guest rooms on the upper floors of the *Ferry Inn* are plainly but stylishly decorated, spotlessly clean, and have comfortable beds. If there's any complaint, it's that internal noise can be a minor problem, and the breakfast is a little disappointing. £££

LINDISFARNE B&B MAP PAGE 28. Off A965, Stromness, KW16 3EX ☎ 01856 850082. A genuinely lovely B&B a short distance outside Stromness, *Lindisfarne* impresses from the very start with a sincerely friendly greeting, attractively decorated and cosy bedrooms, and a homely guest lounge. The breakfast is top-notch, too. Highly recommended. ££

ORKNEY FARM BOTHY MAP PAGE 28. Garson Bothy, Stromness, KW16 3JU ☎ 07802 868690. A cosy self-catering place on the opposite side of the harbour from the centre of Stromness, *Orkney Farm Bothy* is a great spot that somehow feels rustic and modern at the same time. The house boasts comfy beds, a log-burner, and close proximity to the owners' farm animals – make sure to pay a visit to the resident alpacas. ££

ROYAL HOTEL MAP PAGE 26. 55–57 Victoria St, Stromness, KW16 3BS ☎ 01856 850342, W **royalhotelstromness.com**. With a great central location on Stromness' main street, the *Royal Hotel* offers comfortable and attractive rooms. Stromness isn't a generally rowdy place at night, but try to get a room at the back if you're particularly sensitive to noise. Excellent breakfasts are served in the *Haven* downstairs. There's no on-site parking, but it's usually easy to find a spot nearby. £££

West Mainland

AVIEDALE COTTAGE B&B MAP PAGE 34. Rendall, KW17 2PB ☎ 01856 761196, W **aviedalecottage.co.uk**. The two rooms at *Aviedale Cottage B&B* have gorgeous sea views, looking across the channel to Gairsay and Shapinsay, as well as extremely comfortable beds and, in the Thorfinn room's enormous en suite, a lovely bathtub. The owner, Katie, makes a superb breakfast, and is very welcoming. It's also in a very

handy location if you're planning on taking the ferry to Rousay. ££

THE BOATHOUSE MAP PAGE 34. A965, Finstown, KW17 2FH ☎ 07769 216756, W **orkneyself-catering.co.uk/the-boathouse**. *The Boathouse* is an appropriate name: the roof of this self-catering place resembles an upturned boat. With space to sleep up to six people, it's a lovely place with fantastic views of the Bay of Firth, and is in a convenient location offering easy access to Kirkwall. The nearby *Waterside Bistro* is a great spot for breakfast. £££

BUTTON-BEN GUEST HOUSE MAP PAGE 34. Button Rd, Stenness, KW16 3HA ☎ 01856 850794, W **buttonbenguesthouseorkney.com**. A very friendly and welcoming B&B, *Button-Ben Guest House* is in a quiet location on the coast, offering views over to Hoy. There are six attractively decorated rooms here, all en suite, and the breakfasts are very good. The owner, May, is extremely knowledgeable about Orkney and can help you plan your trip, as well as making very fine cakes. ££

CRYSTAL BROOK B&B MAP PAGE 34. Main St, Orphir, KW17 2RB ☎ 01856 811469, W **crystalbrookorkney.com**. You're sure of a great welcome from Sarah and John, the owners of this lovely B&B in Orphir. Rooms are attractively decorated, and there's a lounge for the use of guests, where you'll find snacks and drinks aplenty – relax and enjoy the expansive views across Scapa Flow to Flotta. Breakfasts are truly excellent and generous, and dogs are welcome. Sarah also provides a helpful information sheet, detailing Orkney's sights and restaurants, and times of cruise-ship arrivals into Orkney to help you plan your visit. ££

EVIEDALE COTTAGES MAP PAGE 34. A966, Evie, KW17 2PJ ☎ 01856 751714, W **eviedale-cottages.co.uk**. *Eviedale* offers a pair of excellent self-catering cottages, one sleeping up to three and the other accommodating up to six. Both have very well-equipped kitchens and cosy bedrooms, and the larger one is dog-friendly. There's a very fine bakery and pizza takeaway on site. ££

GRUKALTY MAP PAGE 34. Northside, Birsay, KW17 2LU ☎01856 771281, Ⓦgrukaltyorkneyselfcatering.co.uk. On Mainland's north coast with fabulous views over the Atlantic, *Grukalty* occupies a stunning and quiet location. A self-catering place for up to five people, it boasts a well-equipped kitchen and comfy beds, but its calling card is the glass frontage allowing you to enjoy the scenery, as well as a hot tub on the patio. Great walks from the property lead to the nearby Longaglebe Geo, or a little further to the Brough of Birsay. £££

MERKISTER HOTEL MAP PAGE 34. Russland Rd, Harray, KW17 2LF ☎01856 771366, Ⓦmerkister.com. The *Merkister Hotel* occupies a secluded spot on the shores of the Loch of Harray. The sixteen bedrooms are clean and comfortable, with many of them offering a great loch view. The *Merkister Hotel* is well known for its fishing, and guests at the hotel can hire boats for a half or full day. It's well worth eating at the hotel's restaurant. £££

STANDING STONES HOTEL MAP PAGE 34. A965, Stenness, KW16 3JX ☎01856 850449, Ⓦ thestandingstones.co.uk. A large hotel (for Orkney), *Standing Stones* is home to eighteen rooms, all with lovely comfortable beds, and many with snazzy whirlpool bathtubs. It's in a handy location on the main road between Stromness and Kirkwall, predictably enough near the Standing Stones of Stenness: the best rooms have views taking in the stones. £££

Hoy, South Walls and Flotta

CANTICK HEAD LIGHTHOUSE COTTAGE MAP PAGE 46. Cantick Head Lighthouse, South Walls, KW16 3PQ ☎01856 701777, Ⓦcantickhead.com. A self-catering place with a difference, this cottage in the grounds of the Cantick Head Lighthouse is a wonderful place to base yourself for a couple of days. Set in a beautiful spot in the southeast corner of South Walls, this comfortable and attractive bolthole is equipped with a hot tub, a sauna and a firepit, and you can hire kayaks and paddleboards to get out on the water. It's a lovely and memorable choice. £££

THE NODDLE MAP PAGE 46. B9047, near Lyness, Hoy, KW16 3NU ☎ 07789 516563, Ⓦ airbnb.co.uk/rooms/24725816. An excellent self-catering pad on Hoy's east coast, *The Noddle* offers accommodation for groups of up to ten people. With four bedrooms, a well-equipped kitchen, an inviting lounge with a wood-burner, and a patio with terrific views over Scapa Flow, it makes a perfect base for exploring Hoy and South Walls. Minimum three-night stays may apply in high season. £££

OLD HALL COTTAGE MAP PAGE 46. Off B9047, South Walls, KW16 3PQ ☎01856 701213, Ⓦoldhallcottage.co.uk. Up to six people can stay at the *Old Hall Cottage* near South Walls' Osmundwall Cemetery. The self-catering accommodation offers a fully equipped kitchen, two bedrooms, and a tranquil garden. It's very accessible for guests with limited mobility. ££

RACKWICK HOSTEL MAP PAGE 46. Rackwick, Hoy, KW16 3NJ ☎01856 850907, Ⓦorkney.gov.uk/Service-Directory/S/rackwick-outdoor-centre.htm. *Rackwick hostel* is a no-frills option, but it's a good choice if you're on a budget: it's clean, comfortable, and has gorgeous views across Rackwick Bay. There are two rooms, each containing two bunk beds, and there's also a kitchen and a common room. £

STROMABANK HOTEL MAP PAGE 46. Near Longhope, South Walls, KW16 3PA ☎ 01856 701494, Ⓦ stromabank.co.uk. This welcoming hotel is pretty much in the centre of South Walls, with views to the sea in all directions. Owners Jade and Chris redecorated it in 2021, leaving the four rooms looking very smart and equipped with lovely comfy beds. Upstairs rooms have skylight windows, allowing you to sleep beneath the stars. Hearty breakfasts are served in the conservatory. ££

Kirkwall

ARDCONNEL MAP PAGE 60. Craigiefield Rd, Kirkwall, KW15 1UJ ☎01856 876786, Ⓦ bed-and-breakfast-kirkwall.co.uk.

Located a short distance outside Kirkwall, *Ardconnel* boasts great views looking back towards the town's harbour. Rooms are clean and spacious, with comfortable beds, and the breakfasts are good. It's around a half-hour walk to the town centre. ££

CASTAWAY GUESTHOUSE MAP PAGE 60. Peerie Sea Loan, Kirkwall, KW15 1UH ⊕ 01856 874856, ⓦ castawayguesthouse. co.uk. An easy fifteen-minute walk from the centre, *Castaway Guesthouse* is a good choice in a quiet part of town. Rooms are clean and comfortable, and there's a good range of options for breakfast. ££

HEATHERLEA MAP PAGE 60. Weyland Terrace, Kirkwall, KW15 1LS ⊕ 01856 879116, ⓦ bandbkirkwall.com. A warm and genuine welcome awaits you at *Heatherlea*, a laidback B&B just ten minutes' walk up from the seafront. The rooms are comfortable and homely, with evocative Orkney-themed artwork on the walls, and the breakfast is delicious. A very strong choice. ££

KIRKWALL YOUTH HOSTEL MAP PAGE 60. Old Scapa Rd, Kirkwall, KW15 1BB ⊕ 01856 872243, ⓦ hostellingscotland. org.uk/hostels/kirkwall. A great budget option around fifteen minutes' walk from the centre, *Kirkwall Youth Hostel* offers accommodation in a choice of private rooms and dorms. Breakfast is available for an additional charge, and there are kitchen facilities on site too. Dogs are welcome. £

THE LYNNFIELD HOTEL MAP PAGE 60. Holm Rd, Kirkwall, KW15 1SU ⊕ 01856 872505, ⓦ lynnfield.co.uk. This rambling hotel at the top of town was built in the 1790s as an extra home for the bishop, and has been extended several times over the centuries, without losing its charm. Rooms have plenty of olde-worlde character, with large wooden, ornate beds. There's also a great restaurant and bar, so you won't have to go far of an evening. £££

ROYAL OAK GUESTHOUSE MAP PAGE 60. Holm Rd, Kirkwall, KW15 1PY ⊕ 01856 877177, ⓦ royaloakguesthouse.co.uk. A friendly and welcoming B&B about half a mile from St Magnus Cathedral, the *Royal Oak Guesthouse* is a good choice while staying in Kirkwall. It's clean, quiet and comfortable, breakfasts are tasty, and the resident cat Winston – rescued by the owners after he was abandoned near the Churchill Barriers – is a delight. ££

WEST END GUESTHOUSE MAP PAGE 58. 14 Main St, Kirkwall, KW15 1BU ⊕ 01856 881201, ⓦ westendkirkwall.co.uk. A real place of two halves, this one. On the one hand, the old and rambling building is looking rather tired and can suffer from internal noise overnight. On the other, the owner Andrew is genuinely friendly and helpful, the location is great, and the breakfast is extremely good – the bacon in particular is delicious. With a good spruce-up, the *West End Guesthouse* could be excellent, while as it is, it offers a decent cost-efficient choice. £

Burray and South Ronaldsay

BANKBURN HOUSE MAP PAGE 68. St Margaret's Hope, South Ronaldsay, KW17 2TG ⊕ 01856 831310, ⓦ bankburnhouse. co.uk. *Bankburn House* is a marvellous property that dates back to 1860, and the place still exudes Victorian grandeur. Mick, the owner, is lovely and welcoming, and the rooms are very comfortable. Breakfast is great too. Charging for electric vehicles is available. ££

BRECKS MAP PAGE 68. Off A961, South Ronaldsay ⊕ 01856 831599, ⓦ brecks-selfcatering-orkney.co.uk. There are two cosy self-catering places on site at *Brecks*: the Barn (sleeps up to six) and the Byre (sleeps up to two). They're both lovely, but the Byre is probably the pick of the two, with its charmingly old-fashioned but modernized aesthetic. The kitchens are well equipped, the beds are hugely comfortable, and pets are welcome. Bookings are for Saturday to Saturday, though outside the summer, shorter stays may be possible. ££

THE MURRAY ARMS MAP PAGE 68. Back Rd, St Margaret's Hope, South Ronaldsay, KW17 2SP ⊕ 01856 831205, ⓦ themurrayarmshotel.com. *The Murray*

Arms is a small and friendly hotel in the centre of St Margaret's Hope. The en-suite rooms are comfortable, though as it's a popular pub, they can sometimes be a little noisy in the evenings. The restaurant is very good, particularly for seafood. ££

OLD SCHOOL B&B MAP PAGE 68. Off A961, Burray, KW17 2SZ ☎ 07746 912819. The friendly and welcoming *Old School B&B* treats guests to a large suite of rooms, including a bedroom, bathroom, lounge and sunroom, and there's a patio from which to enjoy views across to Scapa Flow. Breakfasts are excellent, and the owner Janice has a wealth of local knowledge and can help with your plans. £££

THE SANDS HOTEL MAP PAGE 68. Off A961, Burray, KW17 2SS. ☎ 01856 731298, Ⓦ thesandshotel.co.uk. *The Sands Hotel* is a lovely place offering six en-suite rooms, all with sea views. Rooms are quiet and comfortable, the staff are friendly, and the breakfasts are very good. The restaurant serves great lunches and dinners. £££

Rousay, Egilsay and Wyre

THE TAVERSOE MAP PAGE 76. B9064, Rousay, KW17 2PT ☎ 01856 821325, Ⓦ taversoehotel.co.uk. One of the very few accommodation options on Rousay, *The Taversoe* offers clean and comfortable, if unremarkable, rooms. The gorgeous views over Eynhallow Sound, and the splendid feeling of being truly off the beaten path, are strong incentives for choosing to stay here. Dinner is available in the evenings, though it's advisable to book food in advance. ££

Westray and Papa Westray

CHALMERSQUOY MAP PAGE 82. B9066, Pierowall, Westray, KW17 2BZ, Ⓔ enquiries@chalmersquoywestray. co.uk. Pierowall's hostel is housed in a converted barn and enjoys plenty of excellent facilities, including a good kitchen setup and a friendly common room. With eleven rooms available, all of them either en suite or with private bathroom, and an excellent location on the edge of Pierowall, *Chalmersquoy* is a great budget choice. £

NO.1 BROUGHTON MAP PAGE 82. 1 Broughton, Pierowall, Westray, KW17 2DA ☎ 01857 677726, Ⓦ no1broughton. co.uk. The rooms at *No.1 Broughton* are tastefully decorated, immaculately clean and come equipped with marvellously comfortable beds; most also have great views across Pierowall's bay. Throw in the delicious breakfast, and *No.1* is likely to be the No.1 choice for your stay on Westray. ££

PAPA WESTRAY HOSTEL MAP PAGE 82. Beltane House, Papa Westray, KW17 2BU ☎ 01857 644321, Ⓦ hostellingscotland. org.uk/hostels/papa-westray. This lovely, sparkly clean hostel offers accommodation in six private rooms or two wooden shepherd's huts in the garden, and there's also a great common area available for guests' use. It's conveniently located pretty much in the centre of the island, right next to the shop, so it's perfect for self-catering. On Saturdays, it hosts a pub and often live music performances. £

PIEROWALL HOTEL MAP PAGE 82. B9066, Pierowall, Westray, KW17 2BZ ☎ 01857 677472, Ⓦ pierowallhotel.co.uk. Occupying a great location in the centre of Pierowall and enjoying fine views across the harbour, the *Pierowall Hotel* offers six clean and comfortable rooms at very reasonable prices. It's a popular pub, so sometimes rooms can be a little noisy until closing time; if you like an early night, it may not be ideal, but otherwise it's a good choice. £

THE REID HALL MAP PAGE 82. B9066, Pierowall, Westray, KW17 2DB ☎ 07796 998410, Ⓦ braeheadmanse.co.uk. There are just two bedrooms at this lovely place, as well as a large kitchen/diner/lounge, which is entirely at guests' disposal. The building was once the village hall, and sits a short distance outside Pierowall. Comfortably straddling the gap between a B&B and self-catering accommodation, it's a great spot to base yourself for a longer stay. ££

TAMMIE NORRIE COTTAGE MAP PAGE 82. Off B9066, Rapness, Westray, KW17 2DE Ⓦ airbnb.co.uk/rooms/48916242.

Situated at Westray's southern end, *Tammie Norrie Cottage* is a very good place to stay if you're planning on walks around the gorgeous coast. Offering excellent self-catering accommodation for up to two people, it's perfect for a relaxing getaway. ££

Northern Isles

AYRE'S ROCK HOSTEL & CAMPSITE MAP PAGE 102. Coo Rd, Sanday, KW17 2AY ☎ 01857 600410, ⓦ ayres-rock-hostel-orkney.com. This deservedly popular spot on the west coast is a great choice for a stay on Sanday: take your pick from the clean and comfortable hostel rooms, the self-catering cottage, or the stylish camping pods; wild campers are also welcome. The site overlooks the gorgeous Bay of Brough, affording fantastic sea views. The friendly owners also hire out equipment for activities, including sea kayaking and kitesurfing. £

BIRD OBSERVATORY MAP PAGE 104. Twingness, North Ronaldsay, KW17 2BE ☎ 01857 633200, ⓦ nrbo.org.uk. The best place to stay on North Ronaldsay is the *Bird Observatory*, which offers a choice of accommodation: there's a guesthouse, a hostel and a campsite. The stylish guesthouse is perhaps the pick of the bunch, but the hostel is excellent too, while campers can make use of the hostel facilities. It's hard to go wrong, whichever option you choose. Meals are also available at the observatory, and it is home to a reasonably lively pub in the evenings. £

BRAESWICK B&B MAP PAGE 102. Braeswick, Sanday, KW17 2BA ☎ 01857 600708, ⓦ braeswick.co.uk. An absolute gem of a B&B, *Braeswick* has three comfortable rooms, all en suite. Breakfast, which is excellent, is served to guests in a dining room with a stunning view overlooking Sanday's coast. There's a telescope available for guests wishing to take advantage of the clear skies, and the owners will wake you – upon request – if the Northern Lights are sighted. And, last but not least, the resident dogs – particularly Angus – are delightful. ££

EDAY HOSTEL MAP PAGE 96. B9063, London Bay, Eday, KW17 2AB ☎ 07789 900950, ⓦ hostellingscotland.org.uk/hostels/eday. The *Eday Hostel* offers decent kitchen facilities, a good common room, and comfortable beds. Camping on site is also an option. It's generally unstaffed so it's best to book in advance, rather than just turning up. £

FISH MART CAFÉ AND HOSTEL MAP PAGE 98. Whitehall, Stronsay, KW17 2AR ☎ 01857 616401, ⓦ stronsaycafehostel.weebly.com. This very good hostel next to Stronsay's ferry terminal is housed in the former fish market and, today, it's the ideal place to stay. The four rooms offer accommodation for up to ten people, and there's a common room and kitchen too – though with the excellent attached café, you may not feel the need to use the latter. Laundry facilities and towel hire attract an extra charge. £

MILLHAEFEN LODGES MAP PAGE 96. Off B9063, Eday, KW17 2AB ☎ 07810 895075, ⓦ millhaefenlodges.com. *Millhaefen Lodges* is a great overnight stay on Eday, with a string of holiday lodges overlooking idyllic Mill Bay. They're ideal for self-catering, with good kitchens and a convenient location just ten minutes from the island shop on foot. The bedrooms are also very comfortable. £

QUOYAYRE MAP PAGE 102. Elsness, Sanday, KW17 2BL ☎ 01857 600348. The self-catering two-bedroom cottage at *Quoyayre* provides accommodation for up to six people, and there's a well-equipped and stylish kitchen. The location is stunning: it's found on the causeway leading to Quoyness Chambered Cairn, with easy access on foot to beautiful beaches in either direction. Two-night minimum stay applies. £

STOREHOUSE B&B MAP PAGE 98. Whitehall, Stronsay, KW17 2AR ☎ 01857 616263. A lovely B&B in Stronsay's Whitehall village, *Storehouse* has a couple of comfortable bedrooms, as well as a lounge for guest use. Breakfasts are excellent, and evening meals are available on request too. Cash only. ££

ESSENTIALS

Ferries are Orkney's most useful form of transport

Arrival

As an archipelago off the north coast of Scotland, Orkney is accessible by a limited number of routes. Getting here is unlikely to be quick, given Orkney's remote location, so you'd be best advised to put aside a day or even two for travel.

By air

The quickest and easiest way to reach Orkney is by air. **Loganair** (⊕loganair.co.uk) operates all flights in and out of **Kirkwall Airport**, which can be reached by direct flights from Edinburgh, Glasgow, Aberdeen, Inverness or London City. Other than the London route (3hr), these flights take no longer than 90 minutes, making them a speedy way to get to Orkney, but on the flipside, they're not cheap, with prices of at least £100 one-way, and usually a fair bit more. The other downside of arriving by air is that you'll then need to hire a car in Orkney or rely on public transport on the islands, thus either adding extra expense or accepting that your ability to explore the islands may be limited.

By ferry

Numerous ferry routes operate into Orkney; the most common is the **NorthLink Ferries** (⊕northlinkferries.co.uk) route that runs between Scrabster and Stromness up to three times a day, costing around £20 per passenger, plus approximately £60 for a vehicle. This route takes about 90 minutes and treats passengers to a great view of the west coast of Hoy, including the Old Man, on the way.

NorthLink also runs ferries between Aberdeen and Kirkwall, taking six hours and costing £35 per passenger plus £120 for a vehicle, and between Lerwick (on Shetland) and Kirkwall, which takes five and a half hours and

costs £20 per passenger, plus £90 for a vehicle. These routes run every other day.

Other operators include **Pentland Ferries** (⊕pentlandferries.co.uk), which runs a thrice-daily service between Gills Bay on the Scottish mainland and St Margaret's Hope, taking one hour and costing £17 per passenger, plus £40 for a vehicle. **John O'Groats Ferries** (⊕jogferry. co.uk) operates a foot passenger-only service from John O'Groats to Burwick, taking just 40 minutes and costing £16. The downside is that there's no public transport serving Burwick, though the ferry company does lay on a bus to Kirkwall for an additional £4.

Reaching the ferry terminals

If travelling to Orkney by ferry on any line other than the Aberdeen-to-Kirkwall route, you'll need to make your way up to Thurso on Scotland's northeast coast. By car, this is an easy and scenic – if long – drive that involves taking the A9, which begins around Stirling and passes through the Cairngorms National Park and Inverness.

If you're travelling on public transport, your best bet is to take the train to Inverness, where you can pick up the ScotRail service to Thurso. There are four trains a day from Inverness to Thurso, costing around £25 and taking four hours. Alternatively, you could pick up the Stagecoach X99 bus service from Inverness Bus Station: two buses run a day, also taking about four hours and costing £15. The advantage of the X99 is that if you take the 2pm departure from Inverness, you can ride the bus all the way to Scrabster and arrive in time for the 7pm ferry. Any other public transport route to Thurso will leave you needing to make your own way to whichever ferry terminal you're using; taxis are probably your best bet in this scenario.

Getting around

Travelling by public transport is one option in Orkney, though a visit to the islands is likely to be more satisfying if you have some way of getting around under your own steam, whether that be by **car** or **bike**. **Bus** services cover a reasonable chunk of Mainland, but you'll need to plan carefully to make the best use of your time. Naturally, **inter-island ferries** will be hugely useful to you, whether you've got your own transport or not.

Driving
Orkney has an extensive road network, which for the most part is two-lane, though you won't find any stretches of dual carriageway here. Roads are almost always well paved and maintained, though there are a couple of places that require a drive along a bumpy track – Quoyness Chambered Cairn on Sanday, for example. Even where roads are narrow, passing places are common, and you're unlikely to meet another car anyway, as traffic is extremely light.

    Parking is easy to find, and almost always free, the major exceptions being Kirkwall and Stromness, where you'll need to pay if you want to park right in the centre. It's not generally necessary to do this, though, as in both cases, there are free car parks less than ten minutes' walk from the centre. In Kirkwall, the best such car park is found on the seafront next to the Shapinsay Ferry Terminal, and in Stromness, it's on Ferry Rd to the north of the NorthLink Ferry Terminal.

Buses
Bus routes are largely limited to Mainland and across the Churchill Barriers as far as St Margaret's Hope on South Ronaldsay. Operated by **Stagecoach** (ⓦstagecoachbus.com), services are not enormously frequent: check the timetables, which are available online. An all-day ticket costs £9.30, with group discounts available. Stagecoach also offers a hop-on, hop-off service, the **T11**, which swings by many of the Mainland's major tourist sites and costs £16 for an all-day ticket.

    Some of the islands offer a bus service that operates on demand for ferry passengers; Westray's is particularly helpful, with a service that transports passengers returning from Papa Westray on the afternoon ferry down to Rapness in time for the evening ferry back to Kirkwall. It's also possible to book in advance bus transport on Sanday to take you from the ferry terminal to any roadside point on the island. Check ⓦorkney.gov.uk/Service-Directory/B/Bus-Services.htm for booking details.

Bus routes
Particularly **useful bus routes** include the X1, which runs from St Margaret's Hope to Stromness via Kirkwall; the #2, which links Kirkwall and the Houton ferry for Hoy; the #5, which runs from Stromness to the Houton ferry; the #6, which links Kirkwall and Birsay, via the Tingwall ferry for Rousay, Egilsay and Wyre; and the #8S, which runs between Stromness, Skara Brae, the Ring of Brodgar and Maeshowe.

Cycling
Orkney is well suited to **cycling**, given its extensive network of well-

maintained roads. By and large, the islands aren't enormously hilly either, so it's generally easy-going by bike. You won't find many dedicated cycle lanes, but Orkney is not subject to heavy traffic. The only road that tends to be busy is the A965 linking Kirkwall and Stromness, so it's worth avoiding this where possible.

Bikes and e-bikes can be hired at numerous locations across Mainland and on most of the islands; in some cases, there's no charge. If you are relying on bike hire on arrival on any island, it's worth booking in advance. Details of **bike-hire outlets** can be found at ⓦ orkney.com/things/leisure/cycling. It's free to take a bike on any of the inter-island ferries.

Walking

Orkney is blessed with a gorgeous coastline, many sections of which are perfect for keen **walkers** to tackle. Westray, in particular, is an excellent destination for hikers; the Noup Head loop (see page 87) and the Castle o'Burrian coast (see page 81) are both especially spectacular. Those looking for a challenge may want to consider the steep ascent of Ward Hill on Hoy (see page 45), which is Orkney's highest point and affords excellent views, though it's by no means an easy walk. Orkney's major walking route, though, is the St Magnus Way (see page 79), a multi-section hike that follows a path around Mainland taking in spots of historical significance as well as scenic areas. Several other recommended walking routes can be found at the website ⓦ orkney.com/things/leisure/walking.

Ferries

Orkney's most useful form of public transport, the inter-island ferries are a godsend for visitors hoping to explore beyond Mainland. All routes are operated by **Orkney Ferries** (ⓦ orkneyferries.co.uk) and can be booked online. Prices are reasonable, costing £5.50 for a passenger, plus £13 for a vehicle. A couple of services (Stromness to Hoy and Westray to Papa Westray, for example) are foot-passenger only. Note that you will need to reverse onto some ferries, such as the Kirkwall to Shapinsay route, which can be challenging given the angle of the pier, but staff will guide you. It's always worth prebooking, to ensure you don't get marooned on an island, but staff are generally flexible if you find you want to travel on a service earlier than the one you have booked.

Air

Many of the outer islands can be reached by plane, with **Loganair** (ⓦ loganair.co.uk) operating regular services out of Kirkwall and between the islands. Taking an inter-island flight is a real experience – the planes are generally small eight-seaters, and you'll be sat right behind the pilot with fabulous views as you take off and land. The most famous route, of course, is Westray to Papa Westray, which, at two minutes in duration, is the world's shortest scheduled flight. Fares are low (about £36 return, with prices lowered if you stay at least one night on the island) and popular routes do get snapped up, so make sure to book in advance.

Directory A-Z

Accessible travel

Orkney does present a few challenges for travellers with disabilities.

Though there are good paths allowing **accessibility** at several of the top sights – Skara Brae, for example –

this is by no means universal. Most car parks have reserved spaces for disabled visitors, but where **public transport** is concerned, accessing buses and ferries can be challenging – though it must be said that the staff are almost unfailingly willing to help.

Children

Orkney is perhaps not the most obvious destination for children, though there are several attractions that will keep kids entertained. On a sunny day, the sandy beaches are perfect for paddling, particularly those on Sanday, Stronsay and Westray; Evie is a good choice if you're not leaving Mainland.

History-minded children will enjoy trips to the neolithic ruins, as well as the impressive Noltland Castle (see page 85) on Westray. In addition, several museums do make an effort to be engaging for kids: The Orkney Museum (see page 56) in Kirkwall is a good choice, as is the Kirbuster Farm Museum (see page 38) and the Scapa Flow Museum on Hoy (see page 49). Other kid-friendly attractions in Orkney include the Fernvalley Wildlife Centre (see page 40) or, to see wildlife out in the open, spotting puffins at Westray's Castle o'Burrian (see page 81) is a winner.

Children are almost always welcome at pubs and restaurants, as well as at most accommodation, though occasionally B&Bs will not accept anyone under twelve years old, so it doesn't hurt to check at time of booking. The plentiful self-catering options in Orkney are perhaps the best choice when holidaying with children, though camping is also likely to be a memorable adventure.

Cinema

Orkney's main cinema is found at **The Pickaquoy Centre** (Muddisdale Rd, Kirkwall, KW15 1LR ⓟ01856 879900, ⓦpickaquoy.co.uk) in Kirkwall, at which you can see the latest blockbusters and the occasional simulcast of theatre or music events. **West Side Cinema** (10 Church Rd, Stromness, KW16 3BA ⓦwscinema.wordpress.com) in Stromness, housed in a converted church, hosts fortnightly screenings of world cinema, and asks the audience to rate the film using the 'Pingpongometer' afterwards.

There are also monthly film nights at the **Cromarty Hall** (Cromarty Sq, St Margaret's Hope, KW17 2TP ⓦfacebook.com/CromartyHall) in St Margaret's Hope and the **Gable End Theatre** (B9047, Hoy, KW16 3NX ⓦfacebook.com/Gable-End-Theatre-112981545403802) on Hoy.

Crime and emergencies

Orkney is a generally **safe place**, and you're unlikely to have any need for the **emergency services**, but it's always advisable to stay alert. If you need them, you can contact the police, fire brigade, ambulance or coastguard on ⓟ999, or in non-emergency cases ⓘ111 (ⓘ112 for the coastguard).

Discount passes

Many of Orkney's historic sites are operated by Historic Environment Scotland (ⓦhistoricenvironment. scot). Entry to the vast majority of them is free, but where charges apply (notably at Skara Brae and Maeshowe), Historic Environment Scotland members enter for free. English Heritage (ⓦenglish-heritage. org.uk) and Cadw (ⓦcadw.gov.wales) members are entitled to half price entry if it's within one year of joining, or free entry if longer.

Electricity

The current is 240V AC. North American appliances will need a transformer and adaptor; those from Europe, South

4

Africa, Australia and New Zealand only need an **adaptor**.

Health
There's just the one hospital in Orkney, the **Balfour**, which is found in Kirkwall (Foreland Road, Kirkwall, KW15 1NZ ☎ 01856 888100, ⓦ ohb.scot.nhs.uk/home). It has an **A&E**, as well as a good range of non-emergency services. There are GP surgeries on most of the larger islands – a list can be found at ⓦ ohb.scot.nhs.uk/service/gp-practices – though dentists are limited to Kirkwall and Stromness. **Pharmacies** are found only on Orkney's Mainland, although it's often possible to obtain minor medications such as paracetamol from general stores on the islands.

Internet
Signal strength isn't always the best but, by and large, you'll be able to access the internet on your phone from most places on the Orkney Mainland. The islands are a different story altogether, with **internet access** being sporadic at best on many of them. If you're relying on having access to specific information, consider downloading it to your phone before setting off. In particular, use

mapping apps that allow you to download offline copies.

Left luggage
There are no dedicated left-luggage services in Orkney, but in most cases, your **accommodation** will be happy to hold onto your bags for the day after you've checked out, if need be.

LGBTQ+
Orkney is a generally tolerant place for the LGBTQ+ community, but the scene is pretty understated. There's an annual **Pride event** (ⓦ facebook.com/prideorkney), which boasts of being the UK's northernmost.

Lost property
Orkney's **police** have an interactive **online form** (ⓦ scotland.police.uk/secureforms/lost-property) to complete if you have lost something.

Money and banks
Britain's currency is the **pound sterling** (£), divided into 100 pence (p). Coins come in denominations of 1p, 2p, 5p, 10p, 20p, 50p, £1 and £2. Most of Orkney's cash machines will dispense Scottish banknotes, which come in denominations of £1, £5, £10, £20, £50 and £100, though the £1 note is now rarely seen. The £100 note was

---

Public holidays
Public holidays (Bank Holidays) observed in Orkney are:
January 1
January 2
Good Friday
First Monday in May
Last Monday in May
First Monday in August
November 30
December 25
December 26
Note that if January 1, January 2, November 30, December 25 or December 26 fall on a Saturday or Sunday, the next weekday becomes a public holiday.

Accommodation price codes

Each **accommodation** reviewed in this Guide is accompanied by a **price** category, based on the cost of a standard **double room** for two people in high season. Price ranges include **breakfast**, unless stated otherwise.

£	under £75
££	£75–£110
£££	over £110

introduced in May 2022, but at time of writing was not particularly common. £100 and £50 notes are sometimes met with suspicion by traders.

Generally speaking, **contactless** or chip-and-pin card payments are accepted everywhere, though in some cases, you're still going to need cash. **ATMs** and banks can be found easily in Kirkwall and Stromness and on some of the islands, but it's wise to take cash with you when leaving the Mainland.

Opening hours

Opening hours in Orkney can be wildly variable. **Shops** in Kirkwall and Stromness tend to keep relatively standard hours, and are generally open Monday to Saturday between 10am and 4pm at the least, and pubs and **restaurants** usually serve food between noon and 3pm, and then again from 6pm to 9pm. Elsewhere, opening times can be pretty limited, particularly on the islands; it's best to double-check before travelling if you hope to eat in a particular place. Several attractions close entirely over the winter, though most operate round the year with reduced hours.

Post offices

Post offices are found in all the main settlements on **Mainland**, and on almost all of the **islands**, where you'll find the post office in the island shop. Hours can be sporadic, with some branches only open a couple of afternoon a week, though others may be open Monday to Friday between 9am and 5pm. Specific branch opening hours can be checked online at ⓦ postoffice.co.uk/branch-finder.

Price codes

Accommodation and restaurant listings throughout this Guide are accompanied by a corresponding price code; see boxes, above and page 126.

Smoking

Smoking is illegal in all indoor public spaces in Orkney, including public transport, museums, pubs and restaurants. It is also illegal to smoke in a private vehicle if there is a person under the age of 18 in the vehicle. Vaping (e-cigarettes) is not covered by either of these laws, but it is banned on public transport, and individual establishments have the right to prohibit it on their premises.

Time

Greenwich Mean Time (GMT) – equivalent to Coordinated Universal Time (UTC) – is used from the end of October to the end of March; for the rest of the year, Britain switches to **British Summer Time** (BST), one hour ahead of GMT. GMT is five hours ahead of the US Eastern Standard Time and ten hours behind Australian Eastern Standard Time.

Tipping

There are no specific rules, but staff in **restaurants** will usually

Eating out price codes

Each **restaurant** and **café** reviewed in this Guide is accompanied by a **price** category, based on the cost of a **two-course meal** (or similar) for one, including an alcoholic drink:

£	under £10
££	£10–£25
£££	£25–£40
££££	over £40

expect a ten to fifteen percent tip. This tends to apply less in **pubs** and **cafés** where you pay for your food in advance, though in these places you may find a jar by the till for tips. Note that some bills, usually in the more upmarket places, will include a discretionary service charge – you are not obliged to pay this, particularly if you felt the food or service wasn't up to scratch.

Toilets

Public toilets are relatively common across Orkney: they're found at many car parks, in towns and villages, and at ferry terminal waiting rooms. There's no charge for using them.

Tourist information

There are very few dedicated **tourist offices** in Orkney. The most prominent is the iCentre in **Kirkwall** (West Castle St, Kirkwall, KW15 1GU ⓦvisitscotland.com/info/services/ kirkwall-icentre-p333251; daily 9am–5pm), where the knowledgeable staff can help with plans for your visit to Orkney. There's also an RSPB information point here.

For online information, the official Orkney tourism **website** (ⓦorkney.com) is excellent, with news articles, extensive lists of activities, sights and events, recommended itineraries, and an accommodation finder.

Festivals and events

Orkney Folk Festival

May ⓦorkneyfolkfestival.com
Held in venues all across the archipelago, though largely centring around Stromness, the Orkney Folk Festival is a long weekend of folk music performances. Artists include local performers, as well as musicians from across Scotland and beyond.

St Magnus Festival

June ⓦstmagnusfestival.com
The big event in Orkney's calendar is St Magnus Festival, a week-long programme of cultural events featuring music, theatre, dance, poetry, talks, and much more. Performances take place in venues all around Orkney,

though the majority of them are held in Kirkwall or Stromness.

Regattas

July
Several communities, including Longhope and Westray, hold sailing regattas in July. The races are friendly but competitive, and are often followed up by social events such as dances and barbecues.

Orkney County Show

August ⓦorkneycountyshow.co.uk
The Orkney County Show, held on the second Saturday of August in Kirkwall's Bignold Park, is a fun event

with a wide variety of things to see and do – there's show-jumping, a ploughing competition, dance and music performances, craft stalls, and bird-of-prey demonstrations. Definitely worth a visit.

Island Shows

August
Many of the islands, including Sanday, Stronsay and Shapinsay, hold smaller-scale shows, similar in programme to the Orkney County Show. These involve dance performances, barbecues, livestock shows and sporting events. Stronsay's show, which is called the Stronsay Massive Weekend, is particularly enthusiastic.

SheepFest

August ⓦ nrsheepfestival.com
One of Orkney's – and perhaps the UK's – most unusual festivals, SheepFest is held on North Ronaldsay and centres around volunteers making repairs to the island's drystone wall, with frequent breaks for entertainment fixtures such as traditional island dances, an islanders versus visitors football match, and craft workshops. It's a great way to get a flavour of island life.

Boys Ploughing Match

August ⓦ facebook.com/South-Ronaldsay-Boys-Ploughing-Match-247895212016557

A unique event held on the Sands of Wright near St Margaret's Hope on South Ronaldsay, the annual Boys Ploughing Match involves children, rather than horses, competing to plough an area of the beach. Emphasis is placed on the quality rather than speed of the ploughing, and it's worth attending to see the elaborate costumes worn by the competitors.

Orkney International Science Festival

September ⓦ oisf.org
The Orkney International Science Festival consists of a week-long eclectic programme of events, from astronomy sessions and vintage car rallies to art and photography exhibitions and classical music concerts in St Magnus Cathedral. There are also talks on a wide range of topics, from Orkney's geological formation to future sustainability, and everything in between.

Orkney Storytelling Festival

October ⓦ orkneystorytellingfestival.co.uk
Held in several locations across the islands, the Orkney Storytelling Festival seeks to preserve the archipelago's oral heritage. Expect performances of folk tales, including the Orcadian creation myth of Assipattle and the Mester Stoor Worm.

Chronology

c. 3700 BC Construction of the Knap of Howar, Northern Europe's oldest stone house

c. 3100 BC Construction of Skara Brae, Maeshowe, and the Stones of Stenness

c. 2500 BC Ring of Brodgar erected

c. 200 BC Brochs, such as Midhowe and Gurness, are built across Orkney

43 AD According to the Roman writer Orosius, Orkney's rulers submit to the Roman Empire, though there is no evidence of any Roman presence in Orkney

c. 600 Orkney is fully incorporated into the Pictish kingdom, with important settlements established across the island, including on the Brough of Birsay

875 Orkney conquered by the Norwegian king Harald Fairhair, ushering in the Norse era

995 According to the Orkneyinga Saga, Earl Sigurd Hlodvisson converts to Christianity, followed by the entirety of Orkney

1014–64 Rule of Earl Thorfinn the Mighty, under whom Orkney was a powerful territory

1117 Earl Magnus betrayed and martyred by his cousin Hákon

1135 Magnus canonized; he will eventually become Orkney's favourite saint

1137 Construction of St Magnus Cathedral begins

c. 1200 The Orkneyinga Saga is written in Iceland

1472 Orkney is transferred from the Kingdom of Norway to the Kingdom of Scotland

c. 1560 Gilbert Balfour builds Noltland Castle on Westray

1593 Patrick Stewart becomes Earl of Orkney, quickly acquiring notoriety for his cruelty and injustice

1707 Act of Union results in Orkney becoming part of the new Kingdom of Great Britain

1725 John Gow enjoys a brief career as a pirate around Orkney, before being captured and executed

1746 After supporting the Jacobite revolts, Orkney is retaken by the British government

c. 1800 Headland on Hoy's west coast collapses, forming the Old Man of Hoy

1814 Walter Scott visits Orkney and is inspired to write *The Pirate*

1904 Scapa Flow chosen as the base for the British Grand Fleet

1916 HMS *Hampshire* sinks off Marwick Head, with the Secretary of State for War, Earl Kitchener, among the casualties

1919 The German fleet scuttles itself in Scapa Flow

1939 A German U-boat enters Scapa Flow in the first weeks of World War II, sinking HMS *Royal Oak*

1940–44 Construction of the Churchill Barriers, linking Mainland with Burray and South Ronaldsay

1943–44 Construction of the Italian Chapel on Lamb Holm

1966 First ascent of the Old Man of Hoy, by Chris Bonington, Rusty Baillie and Tom Patey

1969 Longhope lifeboat disaster claims the lives of all eight crewmen on the *T.G.B.* lifeboat

1977 Flotta oil terminal opens, becoming a major oil-processing centre

1997 Along with the rest of Scotland, Orkney votes in favour of the creation of the Scottish Parliament

2014 In the Scottish independence referendum, 67 percent of Orkney's inhabitants vote against independence

2019 Orkney ranked best place to live in the UK by the annual Halifax quality of life survey

2020 Orkney forced into lockdown as Covid-19 reaches the archipelago

2020 All Covid-19 restrictions lifted on Orkney

2022 Tourism numbers climb towards pre-pandemic levels

Language

Language can be a thorny, complex and often highly political issue in Scotland. If you're not from Scotland yourself, you're most likely to be addressed in English, but you may hear phrases and words that are part of what is known as Scots, now officially recognized as a distinct language in its own right. Orkney's local dialect of Scots contains many words carried over from Norn, the Old Norse language spoken in the Northern Isles from the time of the Vikings until the eighteenth century.

Scots

Scots began life as a northern branch of Anglo-Saxon, emerging as a distinct language in the Middle Ages. From the 1370s until the Union in 1707, it was the country's main literary and documentary language. Since the eighteenth century, however, it has been systematically repressed to give preference to English.

Rabbie Burns is the most obvious literary exponent of the Scots language – everybody knows his Auld Lang Syne – but there was a revival in the last century led by poets such as Hugh MacDiarmid. Only recently has Scots enjoyed something of a renaissance, getting itself on the Scottish school curriculum in 1996, and achieving official recognition as a distinct language in 1998. Despite these enormous political achievements, many people (rightly or wrongly) still regard Scots as a dialect of English. For more on the Scots language, visit ⓦ sco.wikipedia.org.

Norn and Norse terms

Between the tenth and seventeenth centuries, the chief language of Orkney was Norn, a Scandinavian tongue close to modern Faroese and Icelandic. After the end of Norse rule, and with the transformation of the Church, the law, commerce and education, Norn gradually lost out to Scots and English, eventually petering out completely in the eighteenth century. Today, Orkney has its own **dialect**, and individual islands and communities within each group have local variations. The dialect has a Scots base, with some Old Norse words, but they don't sound strongly Scottish – indeed, the distinctive Orkney accent has been likened to the Welsh one. Listed below are some of the words you're most likely to hear, plus some terms that appear in place names.

Norn phrases and vocabulary

ayre beach
bister farm
bruck rubbish
crö sheepfold
ferrylouper incomer
geo coastal inlet
haa laird's house
howe mound
muckle large
noost hollow place where a boat is drawn up
noup steep headland
peerie/peedie small
quoy enclosed, cultivated common land
setter farm
voe sea inlet

SMALL PRINT

Publishing Information
First edition 2023

Distribution
UK, Ireland and Europe
Apa Publications (UK) Ltd; sales@roughguides.com
United States and Canada
Ingram Publisher Services; ips@ingramcontent.com
Australia and New Zealand
Booktopia; retailer@booktopia.com.au
Worldwide
Apa Publications (UK) Ltd; sales@roughguides.com

Special Sales, Content Licensing and CoPublishing
Rough Guides can be purchased in bulk quantities at discounted prices. We can create special editions, personalised jackets and corporate imprints tailored to your needs. sales@roughguides.com.
roughguides.com

Printed in Czech Republic

Rough Guide Credits
Editor: Joanna Reeves
Cartography: Carte
Picture editor: Tom Smyth
Layout: Pradeep Thapliyal

Original design: Richard Czapnik
Head of DTP and Pre-Press: Katie Bennett
Head of Publishing: Kate Drynan

About the author

Owen Morton is based in North Yorkshire, and has written or contributed to numerous Rough Guides, ranging from Pembrokeshire to the Philippines. When not exploring the world, he entertains himself by writing a blog about 1980s cartoons. His favourite animal is the wonderfully expressive and permanently furious manul, native to Central Asia and sadly not Orkney. Follow him on Instagram at @owenmortonmanul.

Acknowledgements

Owen would like to thank the fantastic team at Rough Guides, particularly Jo Reeves. Thanks also to everyone who gave me great Orkney travel tips: Andrew Morton, Chris Clark, Martin Brasher, James Millington, and no doubt many other people who have managed to slip my mind. It would be a very long list here if I were to thank everybody on Orkney who welcomed me warmly to their hotels, guesthouses, cafés and restaurants, but in particular it was a great pleasure chatting with Paul at Richan's Retreat on Westray: thank you for your hospitality. Finally, many thanks to Martin Brasher and travelling companion Katherine Morton for their tireless proofreading.

Help us update

We've gone to a lot of effort to ensure that this edition of the **Pocket Rough Guide Orkney** is accurate and up-to-date. However, things change – places get "discovered", opening hours are notoriously fickle, restaurants and rooms raise prices or lower standards. If you feel we've got it wrong or left something out, we'd like to know, and if you can remember the address, the price, the hours, the phone number, so much the better.

Please send your comments with the subject line "**Pocket Rough Guide Orkney Update**" to mail@uk.roughguides.com. We'll credit all contributions and send a copy of the next edition (or any other Rough Guide if you prefer) for the very best emails.

Photo Credits

(Key: T-top; C-centre; B-bottom; L-left; R-right)

Adobe Stock 1, 2TL, 2BL, 2CR, 5, 11T, 15B, 17T, 20T, 38, 56
Colin Keldie/Orkney.com 42, 43
David Loutit 14B
Emily's Tea Room 54
Fionn McArthur/Orkney.com 15T, 18C, 30, 62, 72, 75, 78
NorthLink Ferries 118/119
Orkney.com 73, 95, 103, 108
Owen Morton 12/13B, 16T, 19T, 19B, 21C, 27, 41, 45, 50, 52, 53, 84, 86, 88, 89, 93, 99

Photoshot 91
Reading Tom on flickr 20B
Shutterstock 2BR, 4, 11B, 12T, 12B, 12/13T, 14T, 16B, 18T, 18C, 19C, 21T, 22/23, 24, 29, 31, 33, 37, 49, 51, 59, 69, 71, 79, 100, 101, 105, 110/111
VisitScotland/Colin Keldie 20C, 21B, 55, 66, 90
VisitScotland/Kenny Lam 10, 63, 64
VisitScotland/Paul Tomkins 17B, 65, 80, 106, 107, 109

Index

A

accessible travel 122
accommodation 112
 Ardconnel 114
 Aviedale Cottage B&B 113
 Ayre's Rock Hostel & Campsite
  113
 Bankburn House 115
 Bird Observatory 117
 The Boathouse 113
 Braeswick B&B 117
 Brecks 115
 Brinkies Guest House 112
 Burnside Farm Bed & Breakfast
  112
 Button-Ben Guest House 113
 Cantick Head Lighthouse
  Cottage 114
 Castaway Guesthouse 115
 Chalmersquoy 116
 Crystal Brook B&B 113
 Eday Hostel 117
 Eviedale Cottages 113
 Ferry Inn 112
 Fish Mart Café and Hostel 117
 Grukalty 113
 Heatherlea 115
 Kirkwall Youth Hostel 115
 Lindisfarne B&B 113
 The Lynnfield Hotel 115
 Merkister Hotel 114
 Millhaefen Lodges 117
 The Murray Arms 115
 No.1 Broughton 116
 The Noddle 114
 Old Hall Cottage 114
 Old School B&B 116
 Orkney Farm Bothy 113
 Papa Westray Hostel 116
 Pierowall Hotel 116
 Quoyayre 117
 Radwick Hostel 114
 The Reid Hall 116
 Royal Hotel 113
 Royal Oak Guesthouse 115
 The Sands Hotel 116
 Standing Stones Hotel 114
 Storehouse B&B 117
 Stromabank Hotel 114
 Tammie Norrie Cottage 116
 The Taversoe 116
 West End Guesthouse 115
accommodation (by area)
 Burray and South Ronaldsay
  115
 Hoy, South Walls and Flotta 114
 Kirkwall 114
 Northern Isles 117
 Rousay 116
 Stromness and around 112
 West Mainland 113
 Westray and Papa Westray 116
air 122
arrival 120
 by air 120
 reaching Eday 95
 reaching Egilsay 78
 by ferry 120
 reaching Flotta 52
 reaching Hoy 44
 reaching North Ronaldsay 105
 reaching Papa Westray 85
 reaching Rousay 74
 reaching Shapinsay 93
 reaching South Walls 50
 reaching Stronsay 99
 reaching the ferry terminals
  120
 reaching Westray 81
 reaching Wyre 79

B

Balfour 92
Barony Mill 38
Bay of London 96
Bay of Swartmill 84
Betty Corrigall's Grave 49
Bird Observatory 106
Bishop's Palace 59
Blackhammer Chambered
 Cairn 75
Braebister Mound 45
Braeside, Huntersquoy and
 Vinquoy tombs 95
Broch and roll 38
Broch of Gurness 39
Brough of Birsay 37
Burnt mounds 103
Burray 66
Burray and South Ronaldsay 66
Burroughston Broch 93
Burwick 71
buses 121
 bus routes 121

C

cafés
 Archive Coffee 64
 Beneth'ill Café 54
 The Daily Scoop 64
 Emily's Tea Room 55
 Eviedale Bakehouse &
  Bistro 43
 Fish Mart Café and Hostel 109
 Jack's Chippy 91
 Julia's Café 31
 The Kirk Café 64
 The Moorings 80
 The Pier Bistro and Takeaway 31
 Polly Kettle 73
 Richan's Retreat 91
 Saintear 91
 The Waterside 43
cafés (by area)
 Burray and South Ronaldsay 73
 Hoy, South Walls and Flotta 54
 Kirkwall 64
 Northern Isles 109
 Rousay 80
 Stromness and around 31
 West Mainland 43
 Westray 91
The Calf of Eday 98
Cantick Peninsula 52
Castle o'Burrian 81
Cata Sand 103
Chambered cairns 32
Chapel of St Tredwell 89
children 123
chronology 127
Churchill Barriers 67
cinema 123
The Clearances 75
crime and emergencies 123
Cubbie Roo's Castle 79
Cuween Hill 41
cycling 121

D

Dingieshowe 61
directory A–Z 122
discount passes 123
diving 27
drinking 7
driving 121
Dwarfie Stane 45

E

Earl Kitchener 36
Earl Patrick 59
Earl Robert's Palace 37
Earl's Palace 57
East of Kirkwall 60
East of Orphir 41
eating 7
 eating on Egilsay and Wyre 80
 eating on Flotta 55
 eating on Papa Westray 90
 eating on Shapinsay and
  Eday 109

Eday 94
Eday Heritage & Visitor
  Centre 94
Eday Heritage Walk 97
Egilsay 78
electricity 123
Evie Beach 39

F

Faraclett Head 78
Fernvalley Wildlife Centre 40
ferries 122
festivals and events 126
  Horse Ploughing Match 127
  Island Shows 127
  Orkney Agricultural Show 126
  Orkney Folk Festival 126
  Orkney International Science
    Festival 127
  Orkney Storytelling Festival
    127
  Regattas 126
  SheepFest 127
  St Magnus Festival 126
Flotta 52
Flotta Heritage Centre 52
Flotta World War II sites 53
Fossil and Heritage Centre 67

G

getting around 121
Grobust Beach and the Links of
  Noltland 86

H

Hackness Martello Tower and
  Battery 51
Happy Valley 32
health 124
Highland Park Whisky Distillery
  60
Hill of White Hamers 52
Holm of Papa 89
Hoxa Head 70
Hoxa Tapestry Gallery 70
Hoy 44
  Hoy Kirk Heritage Centre 44
Hoy, South Walls and Flotta 44

I

internet 124
Isthmus beaches 96
Italian Chapel 66
itineraries 18

J

John Gow 39

John o'Holland's Bothy
  Museum 88

K

The Kelp Store Heritage and Art
  Centre 88
Kirbuster Farm Museum 38
Kirk Tang 96
Kirkwall 56
Kitchener Memorial 37
Knap of Howar 87
Knowe of Yarso Chambered
  Cairn 76

L

Lady Kirk 85, 102
language 129
left luggage 124
Letto Sands 84
LGBTQ+ 124
Longhope lifeboat disaster 49
Longhope Lifeboat
  Museum 50
Lopness Bay 103
lost property 124

M

Maeshowe 33
maps
  Burray and South Ronaldsay 68
  Eday 96
  Hoy, South Walls and Flotta 46
  Kirkwall 58
  Kirkwall and around 60
  North Ronaldsay 104
  Orkney at a glance 8
  Rousay, Egilsay and Wyre 76
  Sanday 102
  Shapinsay 94
  Stromness 28
  Stromness and around 26
  Stronsay 98
  West Mainland 34
  Westray and Papa Westray 82
Midhowe Broch 76
Midhowe Chambered Cairn 76
RSPB Mill Dam Nature Reserve
  93
Moaness beaches 45
money and banks 124
Mull Head 61
  Mull Head walk 61

N

Ness Battery 25
Ness of Brodgar 36
New Kirk 106
Noltland Castle 85

Norn and Norse terms 129
Northern Isles 92
North Papa Westray 89
North Ronaldsay 106
North Ronaldsay Lighthouse
  106
North Ronaldsay's sheep 107
Notable residents 25
Noup Head Lighthouse 86

O

Olav's Wood 70
Old Man of Hoy 48
opening hours 125
Orkney Folklore and Storytelling
  Centre 25
The Orkneyinga Saga 40
Orkneyinga Saga Centre 41
Orkney Wireless Museum 59
Osmundwall Cemetery 51

P

Papa Stronsay 100
Papa Westray 86
Pier Arts Centre 25
post offices 125
price codes 125
public holidays 124
pubs
  Belsair Hotel 109
  Ferry Inn 31
  Helgi's 64
  The Murray Arms 73
  Robertsons Coffee Hoose 73
  Royal Cask Whisky Gin Bar 65
  The Royal Hotel 55
  Smithfield Hotel 43
  St Ola Hotel 65
  The Pierowall Hotel 91
pubs (by area)
  Burray and South Ronaldsay 73
  Hoy, South Walls and Flotta 55
  Kirkwall 64
  Northern Isles 109
  Stromness and around 31
  West Mainland 43
  Westray 91

Q

Quoygrew 85
Quoyness Chambered Cairn 101

R

Rackwick museums 48
Rendall Doocot 40
restaurants
  59° North 108
  Bird Observatory 108

INDEX

Dil Se 63
The Foveran 42
Hamnavoe Restaurant 30
Lucano 63
The Merkister 42
Skerries Bistro 72
Standing Stones Hotel 43
Stromabank Hotel 54
The Taversoe 80
Twenty One 63
restaurants (by area)
  Burray and South Ronaldsay 72
  Hoy, South Walls and Flotta 54
  Kirkwall 63
  Northern Isles 108
  Rousay 80
  Stromness and around 30
  West Mainland 42
Ring of Brodgar 36
Rothieshorm 100
Rousay 74
  Rousay Heritage Centre 74
  Rousay's heritage trail 77
Rousay, Egilsay and Wyre 74

S

Sacquoy Head 78
Sanday 100
  Sanday Heritage Centre 102
Sand Ayre 104
Sands of Wright 70
Scapa Flow
  Diving in Scapa Flow 27
  Scapa Flow Visitor Centre and
    Museum 49
Scots 129
Shapinsay 92
shops 7
  58.8° North 72
  Airy Fairy 108
  Bayleaf Delicatessen 30
  Beach Gallery 54
  Castaway Crafts 42
  Craftship Enterprise 108
  Cream 30
  Emily's Tea Room 54
  Fossil and Heritage Centre
    Shop 72

Ginkgo Gallery 30
Harray Potter 42
Hume Sweet Hume 90
Judith Glue 62
Orcadian Bookshop 62
Sanday Heritage Centre 108
Stromness Books and Prints 30
The Brig Larder 62
The Orkney Furniture Maker 62
Westray Heritage Centre 90
Wheeling Steen Gallery 90
Workshop and Loft Gallery 72
Yellowbird Gallery 42
shops (by area)
  Burray and South Ronaldsay 72
  Hoy, South Walls and Flotta 54
  Kirkwall 62
  Northern Isles 108
  Stromness and around 30
  West Mainland 42
  Westray and Papa Westray 90
Sigurd Hlodvisson 51
Skaill House 29
Skara Brae 27
Smiddy Museum 69
smoking 125
The south 100
South Bay 106
The south coast 96
The southeast 94
Southern beaches 81
South Ronaldsay 69
South Walls 50
The southwest 101
Stan Stone 106
Start Point Lighthouse 104
St Boniface Kirk 88
St Lawrence Kirk 69
St Magnus 57
St Magnus Cathedral 56
St Magnus Church 79
St Mary's Chapel 79
Stone of Setter 95
Stones of Stenness 33
Stromness and around 24
Stromness Museum 24
Stronsay 97
  Stronsay Heritage Centre 97
  Stronsay Craft Trail 100

T

Tankerness Gardens 57
Taversöe Tuick 74
The Clearances 75
The Orkney Museum 56
time 125
tipping 125
Tofts Ness 104
toilets 126
Tomb of the Otters 71
tourist information 92, 126

U

Unstan Chambered Cairn 32

V

Vasa Loch and Agricola 93
Vat of Kirbuster 99
Viking Totem Pole 69

W

walking 122
  Walking from Rackwick to the
    Old Man of Hoy 48
  Walk to Noup Head Lighthouse
    87
Ward Hill 45
weather and climate 6
West Mainland 32
Westray 81
  Westray Heritage Centre 85
Westray and Papa Westray 81
Westside Church 84
Whitehall 97
Whitemill Bay 105
Wideford Hill Chambered
  Cairn 40
Wyre 79

Y

Yesnaby Castle 25